BACKYARD BLAZE

BACKYARD BLAZE

The Outdoor-Fireplace Lifestyle

LISA WOGAN

photographs by JOHN GRANEN

SASQUATCH BOOKS
SEATTLE

Printed in Singapore by Star Standard Industries Pte Ltd.
Published by Sasquatch Books
Distributed by Publishers Group West
13 12 11 10 09 08 07 06   6 5 4 3 2 1

Art Direction and Book Design: Nina Barnett
Photographs: John Granen
Prop/Photo Styling: Michelle Cristalli
Models: Marc Kriger, Josh Yeyni, Betsy Dowling
Location: John Kenyan, Sundance Landscaping

Library of Congress Cataloging-in-Publication Data
is available

ISBN 1-57061-482-2

Sasquatch Books
119 South Main Street, Suite 400
Seattle, WA 98104
(206) 467-4300
www.sasquatchbooks.com
custserv@sasquatchbooks.com

To Charlie, who keeps my fires lit

CONTENTS

Introduction

Even when a fire pit has more concrete than the Guggenheim, an open flame brings out the guitar-playing, rounds-singing camper in all of us. That's because fire is not so much a thing as an event—a self-perpetuating chemical reaction of oxygen and fuel that generates light and heat. It's showy, unpredictable, and more than a little bit dangerous; so, like mosquitoes, we are drawn to it. A smoky, crackly blaze makes us giddy. We poke at a fire. We melt things in it. We stare at it like zombies.

As campfires in the wild outdoors and bonfires on beaches are being regulated into oblivion, some among us have

fashioned homemade fire pits in our gardens or installed chimeneas on our patios. *Backyard Blaze* celebrates these little outposts of light and heat in the urban landscape. The backyard fire offers a break from our ordered, plugged-in existence. It's where we resurrect childish kicks and spawn funky new traditions.

In *Backyard Blaze,* we define the fire-centric lifestyle and set out its parameters and origins—recognizing that anyone who boils coffee over an open flame in suburbia defies categorization. We look at the range of setups for backyard fires, such as rings, pits, and kettles, and provide the essential how-to's of building and starting fires.

Because the unique properties of fire are central to its hold on us, we furnish a primer on its chemistry, debunking certain oldfangled notions. A pocket history provides a nerdy context for drinking beer outside in January.

Although vegging out *is* the quintessential fireside activity, we recognize that whittling, drinking, storytelling, singing, and other customs deserve our attention. Finally, we stake new territory in the discussion of cooking over open flame. Today, too many backyards are in thrall to giant, tricked-out gas grills. We take care of that with a strictly low-tech and individualistic culinary approach.

With tiny backyard bonfires, civilized humans throw off their modern trappings and step into something primordial and rich—without leaving the yard. It's worth consideration and even praise. After all, fire is what separates the ape from the hominid, the raw from the cooked, and my boring neighbors from me.

CHAPTER 1

Fire in the Hole

Some say the world will end in fire
Some say in ice.
From what I've tasted of desire
I hold with those who favor fire.
　　　　—Robert Frost, "Fire and Ice"

From a Pit in the Ground and Back

On cloudy, moonless nights millions of years ago, our furry ancestors huddled on tree branches with nothing to keep the cold and dark at bay. No cheerful blaze. No grilled hyena. No boiled coffee. These were the dark ages well before the Dark Ages.

Since pencils and fully opposable thumbs weren't in the picture yet, we don't have a good record of how this time Before Nightlife came to an end, but we know it happened a very, very long time ago. Recent tests of bones found in a South African cave suggest they were burned in a campfire

between one and one and a half million years ago. This earliest evidence of an intentional blaze puts "fire taming" in the hands of *Homo erectus*—early hominids whose brains were about half the size of our own. (Think about that next time you can't get your fire going.)

At first, *H. erectus* merely lived *with* fire, borrowing from nature by lighting brands off natural burns started by lightning or from lava flows. That fire had to be tended and protected. If the embers went out, a group of designated toughs might raid another tribe and steal its fire.

As technological advances go, fire makes everyone's top-ten list. Early humans used the torch to leave the cave, to frighten off cave bears, to sleep safe and warm in the open, to smoke and preserve meat, and to stay up late grunting and gnawing bones with friends and family.

Even though we knew a good thing when it burned us, it may have taken hundreds of thousands of years to figure out how to start a fire on our own. (Remember, we had smaller brains.) Paleoanthropologists speculate that a man or a woman accidentally stumbled onto the secret of fire, while busy at the important job of banging rocks together or digging with sticks. Eventually, friction produced smoke or a spark and someone got a big promotion.

Just as the material quality of life was improved by fire, there was an existential revolution as well. The night darkness, which had been a shroud, opened up like the recesses of a cave under torchlight. Fire became the alpha and omega of human life. On the one hand, it was a pragmatic technology for cooking, warmth, and tool making. On the other, it was a spiritual command post, an outlet for impulses we didn't know we had. We painted cave walls by torchlight, told stories around the hearth, and used fire as a medium for communing with gods and ancestors. For my money (and that of the ancient poets), we became fully human when we tamed fire.

And before you could say "survival of the fittest," man was standing upright, wearing a gray-flannel suit and smelling of Burma-Shave. Woolly mammoths and saber-toothed cats were extinct. Fire as everyday necessity and host of a deeper life had been edged out by central heating, electric ranges, and television.

But while you can take the hominid out of the cave, you can't take the cave out of the hominid. We missed our open fires, and we've been aching to get them back. We drive hundreds of miles in packed cars for a wood-fed blaze under a canopy of stars—only to discover a burn ban in effect. We send our sons and daughters to summer camp so they can know what it's like to rinse the smell of pine smoke from their hair in a freezing mountain lake.

We embrace do-it-yourself incinerations with gusto (if not always in compliance with the law), burning raked leaves and sticks in autumn bonfires and garbage during the rest of the year. We cook fondue over Bunsen burners, light tiki torches in Minnesota, and set fire to bananas and cherries in the name of dessert. Every year, we pour the GNP of a small country into lanterns, votives, and tea lights for porches and driveways.

All these contrivances pale compared to the mighty barbecue. The grill has been our most serious and sustained effort to resurrect the primitive ideal. For a long time it worked. We could stand with a cold brew in one hand and a sauce-drenched brush in the other, basting a hunk of meat, and nearly forgetting PIN codes and overdue videos. Of course, we screwed up that escape by improving our grills so they are now the size of SUVs with the capabilities of a hotel kitchen.

The permanent solution has been simple and persistent—a bona fide fire. Outside. Mere steps from the back door. Not primarily for cooking. Not a mere ornament. A place set aside for nothing more than flame for its own sake.

Ever since the fifties, a band of architects, landscapers, homeowners, and independent thinkers (sometimes known as pyromaniacs) has insisted on a little fire out back. The five-decade boom in so-called gracious living has been good for the business of channeling ancient spirits through fire. From stone fire pits to repurposed oil drums, urban campfires are cropping up everywhere as a centerpiece for fellowship or solitary meditation.

The wheel of fortune turns. A million years or so after we first perched on fireside stones in bark-and-grass tunics, we are back—in force. The world is unimaginably different and complicated, but we are still mesmerized by the sight of ruby flames reaching toward dark heavens.

A Fire of One's Own

If you burn a fire regularly, or plan to, you don't want merely to clear a spot in the dirt and surround it with stones, like they do in Westerns. That wastes a lot of heat, encourages smoky plumes, scars the earth, and can catch underground roots on fire. You need a container—preferably one that controls sparks, reflects heat, offers plenty of fire views, and funnels smoke away from nearby neighbors (who may not be enamored with your fondness for burning llama dung). But more important than any of these concrete criteria is the intangible—identifying a firepot that gratifies your primal urge for lighting fire in the first place.

Kettle

When you imagine a fire outdoors, do you see it at the center of a traveling caravan, a cheerful hub where a band of wanderers gets loopy and forgets the trials of a long journey? If so, a kettle may be the fire vessel for you. (If you already have a kettle, yours is a gypsy soul.)

Kettles are small, uncomplicated basins sometimes called pits or bowls. Often they look like oversize woks or Weber grills with the legs cut down. They come in a variety of materials, including chrome, stainless steel, cast iron, and hand-hammered copper. Some are lightweight enough to be portable and are fitted with wheels—a nomad's dream.

A broad kettle provides enough space to attempt various fire-lays but, as you would expect, very little smoke control. Generally, they come with rounded spark screens that fit over the top, barbecue grill attachments, and sometimes a pothook.

Fire Pit

If the high plains drifter were suddenly to settle down with forty acres and a mule, the first thing he'd do is dig a hole in the ground and build a fire pit. Nothing fancy, mind you. But a place to burn big ponderosa pine logs, warm the soles of his boots, and think back on all the women left behind. Maybe, eventually, he'd get around to building a house. Then again, maybe not.

Permanent, open, earthbound structures, fire pits are about as close to a campfire as you're going to find in the city. I've seen charming homemade versions, including a shallow stone-aggregate planter set in a pit lined with river rock. The planter was cracked from the heat of fires and looking like a Greek ruin, but worked just fine.

Fire pits are also built above ground in brick, stone, tile, and marble pedestals, which makes feeding, tending, and cooking over fire a lot easier on the spine. As for style, these fire pits run the gamut, but I'm partial to the fifties-ish brick versions that look like a setting from a Rock Hudson–Doris Day movie.

Today, many fire pits are outfitted with natural gas or propane, and some even convert into stone-topped tables. If your taste is a mite more Las Vegas, no worries. There is at least one fire pit that looks like Liberace's idea of roughing it: a gas-fueled pedestal with faux firelogs or flaming lava granules surrounded by a ring of water jets—all controlled by a switch.

Chimenea

Not all outdoor fire containers cater to fantasies of open space and wandering. The chimenea, for example, is all stay in and cuddle—a curvy burner with a homey legacy.

Folks who think about these things—and by that I mean the friendly experts at the Hearth, Patio & Barbecue Association—say the chimenea (Spanish for fireplace) cracked the whole backyard fire scene wide open in the seventies. The term chimenea is used to describe a variety of outdoor burners, but the real thing is shaped like an upside-down turnip with a round firebox topped by a smokestack.

These are efficient operators. The drafting action of a well-built chimenea (sometimes spelled *chiminea*) draws fresh air into the fire through the mouth and drives hot air out through the neck—feeding the flames and producing little or no smoke. Unfortunately, this limits fire views to a single opening, like a traditional fireplace.

Chimeneas originated hundreds of years ago as bread ovens in Mexico and Latin America, and are still used today for heating and cooking in rural villages. In the late seventies and early eighties, they were imported in substantial numbers for the first time.

Unfortunately, the first generation broke easily. Not surprisingly, they weren't built to travel long distances or to tolerate Duluth winters. When a chimenea cracks in Guadalajara, you just pull together some mud and river clay to build a new one. Up north, gringos ask for a refund.

The latest generation of clay chimeneas is faring better. In addition, cast iron and cast aluminum versions are now fairly common. Iron is sturdier and conducts an enormous amount of heat; just don't let kids or shaggy dogs anywhere close. Iron chimeneas are also extremely heavy and have a tendency to rust. Aluminum is lighter, doesn't rust, and doesn't break like clay, but also tends to be more expensive.

Hopping on the success of Mexican firepots (and regulations in some cities that permit chimeneas but not fire pits) are a host of outdoor fire containers that call themselves chimeneas, but bear only a passing resemblance to the original. These include the you-can-have-it-all chimenea/fire pit/grill combo, which has an open firebox with 360-degree flame views. Mounted on top is a dome that helps funnel smoke and sparks into a short stack. Some of these can be modified, like Transformers, into waist-high grills with wood storage below.

FROST RECONSIDERED:
Chimneys, not fences, make good neighbors, especially where property lines are close together.

Fireplace

What the fireplace lacks in spontaneity, it makes up for in gravitas. A fireplace commands a space in a way no other single element can. The term is generic and is used to describe just about anything that holds burning wood, but as far as I'm concerned, you need a firebox, a flue, a chimney, and a damper to qualify. (The brick fireplace to the right has a smoker in the chimney.) Because of all this engineering, a fireplace offers an added measure of safety over kettles, pits, and chimeneas.

Most full-scale fireplaces do not offer the in-the-round experience we love in our campfires, but Rumford fireplaces, in particular, have their compensations. (These are named for Massachusetts-born Count Rumford, a scientist, inventor, and chimney whiz who might have ranked up there with Ben Franklin if he hadn't sided with England during the American Revolution.) Rumford designs feature an unusually tall firebox that reveals flames all the way to their tips and the smoke escaping up into the chimney. Because you are able to see the whole show, these fireplaces create an impression not unlike a campfire.

Advice for Beginning Firebugs

Try something temporary. Choosing a container for fire can be challenging—each style has its seductions. A chef friend of mine began with a starter model, in the same way some people buy starter homes or enter into starter marriages. She purchased an inexpensive, portable, pit-style fireplace from a camping store. It's designed specifically to take on the road, not at all the sort of thing she imagined taking up permanent residence in her meticulous garden. But she's a deliberate person, and she wanted to predetermine if she'd build fires (which she does almost compulsively) and exactly how she would spend her time around a fire (lots of entertaining). It was a good plan. In the end, she bought a kettle with a grill attachment.

Consider downtime. Most containers will host live fire for a tiny fraction of their tenure in your yard. Think about all the time your firepot will be dark and remember that even when it is not lit, an outdoor hearth can offer a warm focal point in the garden or on the patio.

Create a fire-nights journal. Record the pleasures of your backyard fire, especially customs you invent or traditions you learn from friends. Log your favorite wood, firestarters, and fire-lays. Keep track of games, stories, holiday celebrations, and recipes. Your journal will ignite new enjoyments down the line.

CHAPTER 2

The Care and Feeding of Backyard Fire

When a lovely flame dies,
smoke gets in your eyes.
—Otto Harback

How to Build a Fire

In a *New Yorker* cartoon by Danny Shanahan, a henpecked caveman adjusts the flint on his spear as his unhappy cavewife dangles a chunk of meat over a meager flame and whines: "The Taklaks have a huge fire." It sort of sums up the downside of domestic fire, which we want to dispense with right away. Ever since we tamed this scorching element, Eagle Scouts and wannabes have been building bright, even-burning, spark-free blazes that make the rest of us feel inadequate.

It didn't have to be that way. In the course of a million years, we've cracked DNA, split the atom, and managed to perfect at least a half-dozen fire-building techniques. Pretty much anyone can build a proper fire, with the possible exception of my husband, who is regularly foiled by no-fail instant logs.

The key to a top-notch blaze is structure. You want a fire-build or fire-lay that encourages convection and takes full advantage of flames' inherent tendency to reach skyward. With the right framework, even wet or green wood will burn.

Each situation demands its own sort of fire. The choice of fire-build depends on your fuel supplies, the wind, your surface, your purpose (heat, cooking, or atmosphere), and, honestly, your bravado. Where the tepee is mundane but reliable, the pyre is flashy but less certain. It's your call.

A Word About the Fire Maker

Before anyone puts a match to tinder, we need to touch on the psychological underpinnings of the operation. Because a backyard fire is as conniving and potentially hazardous as a three-year-old, someone has to be in charge. That someone is the fire boss, who manages building the fire, keeping it fed, and extinguishing it at the end of the night.

In couples, the role shakes out pretty fast. It's the rare relationship that happily harbors two natural fire bosses. But selecting and maintaining a fire leader in a group is a different matter. Too often, a visitor, an alpha with something to prove, comes along and tampers with a perfectly good fire. Visitors wouldn't dare fill your dog's bowl without asking, but they don't think twice about dropping a couple sticks of fig wood on your carefully crafted log pyramid. Betas bristle. Gammas hand off their pokers and call it quits. And that's not right.

At the turn of the nineteenth century, around the birth of the scouting movement, American campsites were highly organized. A camp council designated an official Keeper of the Campfire, which helped cut down on conflict and forest fires. Of course, the camps also had secret enforcers and head lice, so this may not be the best model.

Truth is, short of creating a "FIRE KEEP-ER" cap or wearing your Firemanship Merit Badge, the best way to keep stray doms out of your fire is to tend such a satisfactory blaze as to automatically rebuff others' attempts at improvement. It's the sputtering, smoky fire that cries open season on a fire boss's self-esteem.

Ingredients

No matter what sort of fire you build, the basic ingredients don't change.

Tinder is anything that can be lit with a match, such as dead, dry pine needles, leaves and grass, wood shavings, and wadded newspaper. With newspaper, avoid using the glossy color pages; they sometimes contain chemicals that are not good to burn.

Kindling is the stage between tinder and fuel. Most kindling includes sticks that range from finger-width to wrist-width. Pieces should be dry enough to break apart with a snap and small enough to catch from a meager flame.

Fuel or fuel wood are the larger pieces of wood that burn for hours. Fuel should be well-seasoned. Read about selecting wood later in this chapter.

Never use charcoal lighter fluid, gasoline, or other flammable substances not specifically designed as a firestarter. The practical reasons for this should be obvious, but paramount among them is safety. Highly combustible fluid gets out of control fast.

For those who approach fire along more metaphysical avenues, the use of lighter fluid or gas is considered bad form. The idea here is that fire is a living spirit to be feared and revered. Building a fire-lay is like preparing your home for a visitor. Lighting the match is the invitation. If you dump gas on your fire-lay, the fire spirit is forced to show himself, which pisses him off. Hence, he flares, burns wildly, and smells bad. An inviting fire-lay built by well-intentioned hands makes for a happy, constant fire spirit.

One final prefatory note: Check the literature that came with your firepot so you know what's best for your setup. For example, new terra-cotta chimeneas require curing in the form of a few long-burning, low-heat fires to strengthen the clay before you burn a really hot fire. Most backyard fireplaces are only safe with a medium-size blaze. Know your limits.

A Fistful of Fire-lays

Tepee

The tried-and-true and most widely taught fire-lay is the tepee. If you learn only one method, this should be it. The tepee is good enough for survivalists, so it's probably good enough for suburban bushmen as well.

1. Picture a tepee before you begin. Clear your mind of Romanesque, baroque, and rococo architecture—that stuff will just get you in trouble.

2. Place a handful of tinder in the shape of a cone in the middle of your fire site. Around that tinder pile, arrange small sticks of kindling as if they were the poles of a tiny tepee.

3. Arrange small- and medium-size sticks of fuel wood around the kindling to create a third tepee, ignoring any bystanders who claim your tepee resembles a yurt. (It helps if the surface of your fire pit is sand or rocks, where small pieces of wood can be wedged for extra stability.)

4. From the windward side, ease a burning match under the tinder. Because you don't want to knock over your lovely tepee, an extra-long wooden match, a long-handled butane lighter, or an uncooked pasta noodle lit by a regular match or lighter works great here. In some circles, using more than one match to start a fire is a sign of failure.

5. The flame from the burning tinder should light the kindling and the fuel wood above. As the tepee burns, the outside logs will collapse inward, feeding the fire and adding drama. Keep adding fuel from the lee side, one piece at a time, in the shape of the tepee. Once the coals are glowing, you can be more ad hoc about feeding the fire. Seasoned fire builders will often light the tinder at step 2 and build the tepee as it burns.

Remember to leave plenty of space for air-flow and to keep the fire small and compact. The tepee works best in fire rings and wide pits, but it makes a good kindling structure for starting fires in fireplaces and chimeneas.

The tepee fire burns well even with wet wood.

If you want to kick-start your fire, try my Yankee stepmother's trick of tossing a candle stub in with your tinder. The melting wax buys you extra burn for catching the kindling.

The tepee may be all we need, but we want the full range of fire-building approaches in our arsenal. We watch *Survivor*. We know that if we can't turn banana peels into fire, we'll be voted off the island. In the following pages are abbreviated instructions for six standard fire-lays. Keep in mind that the fundamentals of building and lighting the tepee apply throughout.

BOY SCOUT TIP:

Leave an opening, like a door, in your teepee on the side facing into the wind. This works like a natural bellows, feeding the flame wtih all-important oxygen.

Log Cabin

In the middle of the pit, make a small cone of tinder. Then place two sticks of kindling parallel to each other, on opposite sides of the tinder pile. Lay a second pair on top of and perpendicular to the first, creating a square. Continue adding kindling until you have a drafty little log cabin with no windows or doors. Lay a few small pieces of kindling across the top. Light the tinder.

PYRAMID

Once the cabin is putting off some nice flame, either lay larger logs in a square close to the fire, like the foundation of a second, more substantial cabin, or lay small pieces of wood directly onto the burning kindling if doing so won't smother the flames.

The log cabin is sturdier than the tepee but not as efficient.

Lazy Man's Log Cabin

This variation on the log cabin starts with two small logs with a pile of tinder between them. Small kindling is laid over the tops of the logs, like a flat roof over the tinder. The tinder is lit, and the kindling catches fire. As it burns, the kindling is broken and pushed down onto the consumed tinder and replaced with more kindling. When the new roof is burning well, it is also pushed down. Eventually, the kindling pile will burn brightly, and the logs will light from it. This is a pyro's delight, because it requires lots of poking and feeding early on.

Pyramid

Sometimes called a friendship fire, the pyramid can be large and low-maintenance, perfect for a long night's coven. To lay this fire, place two small logs or branches parallel on the ground about one foot apart. Place a solid layer of small logs

PERENNIAL PROBLEMS:

The most common mistakes in fire building are choosing poor tinder, failing to shield a fire from the wind, and smothering the fire with too-big pieces of wood.

Pyre

This fire-build has a grim ancestry that makes it a great conversation piece. It's built like the sturdy log cabin but starts with thin pieces and moves up to ever-thicker pieces. The pyre *should* collapse in a controlled manner without restricting airflow. This can be a tricky one so keep it on the small side.

Lean-to

Now we're totally off the grid, or at least out of the fireplace. Push a green stick into the ground at a 30- to 45-degree angle (depending on whom you believe) pointing into the wind. Place your tinder pile under the stick, close to where it meets the ground. Lean pieces of kindling against the lean-to pole. It should look a bit like a Boy Scout shelter from the forties, back when the leadership encouraged environmental sacrilege such as raging bonfires and making comfy beds from fresh-cut pine boughs. As the kindling catches fire from the tinder, lean more against the pole and eventually replace with fuel-size logs.

across the parallel logs, as if you are creating an elevated floor. Add three or four more layers of logs or branches, each layer smaller than and at a right angle to the layer below it. On top of the pyramid, make a tepee-style starter fire of tinder and small kindling. As the starter fire burns, it will ignite the logs below it. Obviously, the pyramid isn't the choice for a breezy night.

This is no casual fire-lay. The pyramid, like its inspiration, is a commitment. Because the fire burns top down, you determine your minimum fuel supply *before* anyone lights a match. If the night's a bust, you may have a hell of a fire to extinguish before bed.

LEAN-TO

Cross-ditch

Cross-ditch is a fairly radical choice in neighborhoods with pristine lawns. It's included in this list for those seeking a new challenge. Dig two trenches in the shape of the letter X.

Each trench should be about a foot long and three inches deep. Put a pile of tinder on the intersection of the cross. You can build pretty much any fire structure here. The shallow ditch allows air to sweep under the fire-lay and provides a flame-boosting draft.

When to Cry Uncle

There will be times when you just can't get your fire-build to roar. Before giving up and suffering rough treatment from your teenage kids, troubleshoot for obvious problems. Billowing smoke? Maybe you left the top on your smokestack, or the flue in your chimney is closed. Also, check for wet or green ingredients. Tinder snuffing out or kindling not catching? There might be some water in the bottom of your pit, or the layer of ash or sand could be damp. Wind getting you down? Forget about fire on gusty days; there's just too much danger in a flying spark. In the case of a slight breeze, create a windbreak with your patio furniture.

If you were in the backcountry and still fireless, it would be time to crank up the gas stove, boil water for hot cocoa, and zip yourself into a down sleeping bag. For the urban fire maven, the equivalent is to chuck the backwoodsman ideal, wander inside, and tap your backup supply of firestarters and Duraflames.

When it's frosty outside, things start to feel dire faster—probably out of all proportion to the situation. But if, like Jack London's frozen prospector in *To Build a Fire*, you're considering slicing open your dog and climbing in for warmth, it's time to cry uncle.

How to Start a Fire

Matches? We Don't Need No Stinkin' Matches

People say they'd love to know how to start a fire without a match. I can't help wondering why. If there comes a time when you desperately need a fire and you don't have matches or a Zippo, you probably won't have a magnifying glass, or a bow-drill, or flint and steel, either—unless you're MacGyver. But if you're MacGyver, you can start a fire with a shoelace and a pizza cutter.

Nonetheless the urge is there. We want to start fires like our ancestors. Maybe because we'll never understand how the Clapper works or what makes a computer freeze. Motive aside, if you take the time to learn these skills (and it takes a lot of time), you're guaranteed to make a lasting impression when you start sawing a bow-drill like some lapsed member of the Cave Bear clan.

Three Ways to Conjure Fire Without Using a Match or Lighter

Tap nature. This requires patience and a good location scout. The idea here is to light your Georgia fatwood directly from the source, so either wait for an opportune lightning strike or wander down to the local lava flow.

Channel the sun. Use glass to focus a concentrated ray of sunlight on a nest of dry tinder. All you need is a sunny day and any convex lens—a magnifying glass, binoculars, a camera lens, telescope sights, even eyeglasses. Hold the lens over the same spot until the tinder begins to smolder. Gently blow or fan the tinder into flame, and apply it to the fire-lay. The bar for this sort of thing was set by Archimedes (287–212 BCE).

During the siege of Syracuse by the Romans, the Greek mathematician and inventor is said to have set fire to enemy ships by focusing the sun's rays on them with a set of mirrors.

Apply elbow grease, aka the fire-by-friction method. There are essentially two primitive friction techniques for starting fire: rubbing flint on steel and rubbing two pieces of wood together. In the former case, the fire maker strikes a flint against high-carbon steel to make sparks. In the latter, wood particles are ignited by the process of rubbing a hardwood drill against a softwood plank.

Because you probably have all the necessary materials kicking around, we're going to tackle a sticks approach, known as the bow and drill or bow-drill technique. There are four homemade instruments necessary for starting fire with a bow-drill. (You can buy kits and instruction videos for glass, bow-drill, hand-drill, and flint and steel fire starting; see Resources, page 130.)

SOCKET
BOW
DRILL
FIRE BOARD
CORD

Drill. Also known as the spindle, the drill should be a straight, seasoned hardwood stick about an inch in diameter and eight to ten inches long. Whittle about an inch at each end into a blunt point.

Fire board. A flat, rectangular board of seasoned softwood about an inch thick, three inches wide, and eight or more inches long. About an inch from one end, cut a V-notch about a half-inch deep on one side of the board.

Bow. The bow is made of a green, straight, flexible (but not nearly as pliant as an archery bow) branch about an inch in diameter and the length of your arm from elbow to fingertip. Notch the ends of the bow and string it. The bowstring can be any type of cordage. A clove hitch works well. The string should be quite taut.

Socket. Also known as a handhold, the socket is stone or bone that feels comfortable in your hand with a slight depression on one side. You can also bore a quarter-inch pit into a piece of hardwood. This socket should cup the top of the drill to hold it in place as you saw. Now you're ready to make fire.

1. Prepare your fire-lay.

2. Nearby, place a thin board or piece of card-board on flat ground. Set your fire board on top of it and a bundle of tinder under the notch in the fire board.

3. If you are right-handed, hold the bow with this hand and place your left foot on the fire board. (Lefties need to reverse these instructions.) Loop the bowstring around the drill once, so that the drill is on the outside of the bow.

4. Place the drill in the fire board notch. With your left hand, fit the socket onto the top of the drill to hold it in position.

5. Press down with the left hand and saw the bow back and forth to twirl the drill.

6. Once you have established a smooth motion, apply more downward pressure and work the bow faster. This action will grind a black powder into the tinder, causing a spark to catch.

7. When there is a lot of smoke from the black powder, you have a spark. Blow on the tinder until it ignites.

Ernest Thompson Seton— artist, outdoorsman, author, and founder of the Boy Scouts of America—once claimed to hold the speed record for the "rubbing stick" method at thirty-one seconds from cold sticks to full glow. If you try to master the bow-drill, you'll appreciate the significance of his accomplishment.

Creating a fire from sticks is extremely challenging for a novice. Some simple tips can help. You must exert much effort and be persistent. It's helpful to hold the drill upright.

Brace the wrist holding the drill in place against your shin, to create a solid foundation. Also, once you see smoke, don't stop sawing until you're sure you have a healthy spark.

A Short History of Matches

Matches have not always been the breezy shortcut they are today. In the late 1820s, an English apothecary created "sulphuretted peroxide strikables." The first friction matches, these three-inch wood splints dipped in sulphur, potassium chlorate, and other nasty chemicals lit when rubbed against sandpaper.

A year or two later, an opportunist named Samuel Jones began marketing the unpatented invention as Lucifers, which became popular with smokers and, in turn, helped make smoking more popular. Unfortunately, Lucifers smelled foul and ignited with explosive ease.

In 1830, a French chemist attempted to improve on the original by creating a match made with white phosphorus, which was odorless but also poisonous. Workers in the match factory and children who sucked on the apparently tasty match tips developed a debilitating bone disease called phossy jaw. It wasn't until 1910 that the Diamond Match Company patented the first nonpoisonous match in the United States.

Safety First

There's no poetry in a fire extinguisher. No passion in a spark arrester. Who really wants to be careful, when what moves us to build fires in the first place is that frisson of elective risk? But where caution fails to inspire, folly gets our attention. The men and women who sell fireplaces for a living seem to understand that. They know as well as anyone how a little thrill can turn three-alarm ugly. If you ask, and sometimes even if you don't, they'll tell you stories of cosmic carelessness that will have you shaking your head at the foolishness of some goofus and ordering a backup extinguisher.

A bridegroom in central Minnesota created a mini-bonfire from gift boxes in his backyard chimenea. The clay firepot cracked from the intense heat, and managed to burn his house down on his wedding eve. Good news: no boxes to haul to the dump. Bad news: no gifts and no bride either.

Then there's the couple who kept a fire going for days in a dirt pit behind their lakeside home in Western Washington. They put it out—they thought—and returned to their city house, unaware that the long burn had caught tree roots on fire. It was kayakers paddling by who noticed the smoldering river bank a day or two later. The neighbors were not amused.

Even seasoned outdoorsmen make mistakes. Consider the group of survivalists in Colorado, skilled in primitive camping techniques, who built a temporary fire ring with river rock. When the stones heated up, the water inside (they're permeable, remember) expanded. The rocks burst, sending fiery shrapnel in all directions.

Usually, disaster has far more modest beginnings. A spark no bigger than a mosquito sails into a pile of dog fur, or day-old ashes dumped in the garden harbor an ember—the rest is chemistry and strapping firefighters.

Eight Ways to Be Sure You Don't Headline the 11 o'clock News

Try not to concede the higher ground to friends who don't have the fire department on speed dial. Remember these simple rules of thumb.

1. Location matters. Site your pit or free-standing fireplace at least ten feet from your house or other structures, including your neighbor's garage. Only a spark engineered by NASA can cover that range. (Some local fire codes specify even greater distances.)

Set your burner on a surface that won't catch fire: cement, stone, or sand. Avoid grass, leaf piles, and pools of gas. For decks, use a lightweight, flexible fiber-cement grill pad under your firepot to protect the immediate area from sparks. Also, overhead, you want open sky, with no low-hanging branches.

2. Sparks can fly. Use a spark screen, especially with pits and kettles. If you plan to cook or roast marshmallows, you'll obviously need to pull back the screen. But if it's blustery, wait until the wind dies down. With smoke-stacks, a chimney-top spark arrester traps and breaks up embers.

3. Sap is sassy. Green wood creates more sparks than dry wood, so be sure your fuel wood is seasoned. Pitch or sap (found in tamarack, cedar, and other pines) also has a tendency to pop. So look out. Manufactured firelogs almost never spark.

4. Starter fluid is a dangerous and wimpy crutch. Besides, after reading this chapter, you'll be able to build and light a fire in a blizzard.

5. It pays to be a little paranoid. Keep a fire extinguisher, a bucket of water, a bucket of sand, or a garden hose nearby. In the case of a fire extinguisher, figure out how to use it *before* there's trouble. It's best not to read the directions by the light of a burning house.

6. Open fire is not a screen saver. Never leave it unattended.

7. Ash is a fantastic insulator. Allow coals to cool for forty-eight hours before clearing them out. If you aren't able to wait, douse the coals with water and stir. Never place coals in plastic, paper, or wooden containers—only metal.

8. Children are flammable. You know it, but they don't. Enough said.

Fire districts have their own rules about backyard fireplaces, and many stipulate brush-free areas, spark screens, fire extinguishers, etc. Find out about your local rules. Also, pay attention to burn bans. Don't light up when fire danger is high or when there's a pollution advisory.

SMART WOOD:

To be sure your wood is seasoned and burns with fewer sparks, buy a freshly cut cord and let it season on your own rack for at least six months. This is also a good way to keep the price down, especially in the spring, when cordwood is usually less expensive.

Every man looks at his wood-pile with a kind of affection.
—Henry David Thoreau, *Walden*

The Wood Supply

Say what you will about the lack of dramatic tension in *Walden*, Thoreau was right about one thing: A woodpile—especially one you chop, split, haul, and stack yourself—inspires devotion. Neat rows of split wood, drying in the wind and sun and perfuming the air with fresh sap, are a monument to the time and energy it takes a tree to grow and the hard work to harvest it. On cold, gray days, the woodpile stands as a promise of cozy nights.

For the most part, we don't cut our own wood anymore. Most of the fuel stacked up in backyards is bought by the cord or half-cord from local firewood suppliers, usually one-man (nearly always men) outfits run by guys who love wood and hate bosses. They find their supply from an ad hoc network of homeowners who want trees hauled away, scrap from logging operations or tree services, and sometimes from their own backyards or woodlots.

The nice thing about buying wood this way is

the local connection. It's like farmers markets or farm co-ops, where the story at the source is part of the pleasure of consumption. Normally quiet, a true woodsman can be expansive on the subject of trees. Become a repeat buyer and you'll discover what it's like to burn the best-cut, best-seasoned wood available.

Mostly, though, we buy our wood in small bundles or boxes, ready-to-use like prewashed lettuce and marinated meat. Corner markets in cities have sold wood in small bundles for ages, but now it's a common sight at megastores in the suburbs. The logs are chopped in uniform, burnable wedges, shrink-wrapped in plastic or bound in cord. There may be no unburnable snags and no black widow spiders here, but sometimes we can't even tell what kind of wood it is.

For aficionados, anonymous wood won't do. These dedicated connoisseurs understand that wood is the heart of the matter. It's obvious but needs to be said: All wood burns; all wood does *not* burn the same way. The choice of firewood dictates the color and size of the flames, the duration of the burn, the crackle and spark, the smoke and the fragrance—and we're not even talking about using wood in cooking here, which raises the conversation to a whole other level of refinement.

In general, what you need to think about with wood is hard versus soft. The hardest wood is often called ironwood; the softest is balsam. Hardwoods include all deciduous trees, such as hickory, oak, beech, and apple. They are generally preferred as heating firewood because they are dense and produce more heat, between 20 and 25 million British thermal units (BTUs) per cord. (Softwood generates 30 to 50 percent less heat.) Hardwood, which can be difficult to light, produces slow, smoldering burns without many sparks.

Softwood—which includes all conifers, such as spruce, pine, and cedar—is less dense and usually loaded with sap. This wood catches fire easily and offers flashy, quick burns, making it perfect for the backyard fireplace. For the same reasons, softwood makes the best kindling. But be warned, woods with a lot of resin tend to pop, so you need a spark arrester and a firebox screen.

Seasoning

Freshly cut wood is "green." It's not good for burning, doesn't give much heat, and produces lots of annoying smoke. Green wood has to be

cut into small pieces and left to "season" in the open air. In six months, the moisture content drops from about 45 percent to between 20 and 25 percent, which is just about perfect. If wood is left to season too long it becomes bone dry, burns too hot and too fast, and produces dangerous sparks. Think of it as cranky, old wood.

To the untrained eye, it can be tough to tell if wood is ready to burn. In general, green wood is heavy and makes a thud if dropped on pavement. Well-seasoned firewood is lighter in weight, with dark, cracked ends. It makes a hollow clunk sound when dropped.

Storing

You've found a wood dealer with a quaint story and some fine orchard wood, but where to store it? The standard cord is 128 cubic feet—which piles up to about eight feet long, four feet tall, and four feet deep—taking up the space of a Mini Cooper, which is a bad analogy, because the garage is just about the worst place you can store your wood.

A pile of wood is like a fancy co-op with an indiscriminate board—welcoming to every hairy or hard-shelled creature you don't want in your home. Carpenter ants. Termites. Wood-boring beetles. For the same reason, you shouldn't even stack it up against the outside of the house, because a termite enjoys a cedar shingle as much as seasoned oak.

Stack wood in a shed or a stylish free-standing rack built for this purpose—off the ground and away from the house. The rack or shed should be covered on top to protect it from rain but open on the sides to allow the wind and sun to dry the wood.

Also, I hope it doesn't have to be said, but if your wood gets bug infested, don't spray it with a pesticide. You probably won't even reach the troublemakers, and burning pesticide-soaked wood creates noxious gas. The best practice is to keep the wood outside, and then simply brush it off when you're ready to bring it inside for a fire.

Disposing of Wood Ash

Before you dump your ashes in the trash, consider putting them to work. Under the right circumstances, they can be a boon in the

garden. Spreading cold wood ashes on flower beds and the lawn enriches the soil in the same way wildfires naturally replenish the forest floor. It's why if our houses, golf courses, lodges, and highways weren't in the way, we'd probably let all forest fires burn themselves out.

Wood ashes are high in essential plant nutrients including potassium, calcium, sodium, magnesium, and phosphorus. As with ground limestone, adding wood ash to soil also increases its pH, making it more alkaline. This can be helpful in regions with high rainfall, where soils are typically acidic. The opposite is true of dry regions, which tend to have more alkaline soil, and where adding wood ash might be a bad idea.

Boutique Firewood

Wood is "boutique" when it's packaged in a burlap bag or sold in cedar crates over the Internet. Generally, this isn't wood you burn for the hell of it. It's moody wood with lots of attitude and backstory. Boutique woods are often praised for their culinary edge in smoking and barbecuing, but there are some that deserve to be appreciated for their pure burning essence.

Piñon (pinyon) pine: If the Old West has a signature fragrance after cow pies, it might be the piney smoke of *Pinus edulis* (Latin for *edible pine*). Found in the West, Southwest, and Mexico, piñon (page 38) is a prized burning wood with smoke that wards off mosquitoes and a scent that gets under your skin. One stockbroker in New York, who experienced piñon pine campfires on a backcountry trip in the Southwest, now imports the wood to his East Coast home.

Juniper: Found on the same dry, rocky slopes as piñon, juniper warmed Anasazi homes 2,000 years ago with a pleasant cedarlike scent and a crackling, popping burn. It makes excellent kindling and chimenea wood. In particular, alligator juniper (*Juniperus deppeana*) has a rough, textured bark like an alligator hide, which burns into bright coals (page 34). One-seed juniper (*Juniperus monosperma*), also called shagbark, has a shaggy coat that looks lovely just sitting in the wood holder (see opposite).

CHILL FACTOR:
Really cold wood can be hard to light.

Mesquite: Though mesquite has been branded into the communal consciousness through misadventures such as mesquite barbecue chips, the shrubby tree was long revered as a source of tea, syrup, folk medicine, and ground meal for the Native Americans of the Southwest. (Coyotes gobble mesquite beans in the summer.) Because it grows in the Texas desert, *Prosopis* has huge taproots. These are chopped up for firewood, which burns hot and nearly smokeless with a sweet fragrance.

Hotsticks: This is the trademarked name for firewood that has been kiln-dried to remove moisture, contaminants, mildew, mold, bugs, termites, etc. At last, a wood for verminophobes. Resourceful fire-lovers can wheedle the kiln-dried scraps (which burn extra hot, since there's a small amount of moisture) for free from wood shops or construction projects. Just be sure to avoid burning treated wood, such as the sort used in decks or landscaping ties.

> **SIZE MATTERS:**
> Larger pieces of wood take longer to ignite and release their energy more slowly. Smaller pieces are good for short, hot fires.

Faux Firelogs

It's easy to be snotty and elitist about wood, to rank faux logs down there with orange juice concentrate and Sanka. But closer inspection reveals that fabricated firelogs have a lot going for them. First of all, no new trees are felled to make them. Second, the materials are almost entirely recycled or reclaimed, which means less waste goes to landfills. Finally, they often burn "cleaner" than the real thing.

There are downsides. No wood-smoke smell. Usually, no romantic crackle. Worst of all, these logs don't require tending. Stoking them with tongs or a poker will just cause them to break up and burn out. That means those of us who use fire tending as an obsessive-compulsive outlet need to look elsewhere.

Duraflame: Created by the California Cedar Products Company as a way to do something useful and lucrative with the sawdust from milling cedar pencil slats, these ubiquitous firelogs are a combination of sawdust, ground nut shells, cardboard, and petroleum wax. In 2002, Duraflame introduced Open Air firelogs for chimeneas and campfires. They are engineered to burn slowly outdoors and to have a "natural woodlike charred appearance," which honestly takes a stretch of the imagination to see. Real wood with all its hassles provides a more nuanced and complicated burn and lasting coals. But Open Air logs do have the secret Crackleflame ingredient, which simulates the sound that is essential for a true fire mood.

Goodwood: These logs are made of pressed sawdust like Duraflame, but without the other stuff, including paraffin binders. Wood, wood chips, and sawdust, collected from mills and woodland cleanup operations, are compressed so densely that the wood's natural lignin (the agent in wood that holds it together) melts and binds the wood particles. Goodwood comes in an unprocessed jute fiber sack, which acts as the tinder. Jennifer Young, who helped create and launch Goodwood out of her garage, calls it "Boy Scout in a bag."

Java-Logs: Invented in 1998 by a Canadian mechanical engineer, Java-Log is a sweet-sounding mix of molasses and spent coffee grounds. Makers of the Java-Log claim that coffee has 25 percent more energy than wood (which is one of many reasons to brew *it* rather than bark). That may be why these logs produce tall, bright flames. Like most other composite firelogs, Java-Log is essentially a set piece and not a significant heat source.

Phat Wood

When it comes to fire, fat is beautiful. "Fat" in this case has nothing to do with girth; it's a way of describing wood loaded with sap, pitch, or resin.

Fatwood is hand-cut kindling that comes from the stumps of Southern pine trees (see Georgia fatwood, page 35). Long after the tree has been felled, an abandoned stump continues to absorb nutrients, which it converts to sap. The elevated sap content makes the wood useless as lumber and highly flammable—creating a spicy-scented, all-natural firestarter. When fatwood burns, sap beads and sizzles on the surface.

While the glories of Southern fatwood are well known, the West's *pitchwood* is just as fat. The highly resinous timber of yellow and ponderosa pine has long been revered by some Native Americans for its combustibility. River guides and scouts use splinters of pitchwood to jump-start campfires. For home use, Lightning Nuggets and Lightnin' Bugs are two petroleum-free firestarters made from recycled, pulverized, compressed pitchwood and a small amount of food-grade wax.

CHAPTER 3

Campfire Mind

*I am for those who believe in loose
delights....*
—Walt Whitman, "Native Moments"

Fireside Do's

All this mucking about in the yard has one overriding purpose, what I like to call Campfire Mind. This is an altered state that can only be achieved around an alfresco blaze, a degree of mellow conjured by dreamy, hot, hypnotic flames in the outdoors. Campfire Mind shouldn't be confused with the way you feel in a hot tub or just before drifting off to sleep. It's more engaged and communal. Peering into timeless fire in the company of friends, half-occupied by conversation, drinking, and stoking, we put the brakes on time—this is Campfire Mind. Certain age-old activities have a way of encouraging and enhancing this dynamic stupor. They help us relax, connect, and channel the unique spirit of urban flambé.

Tipple

Booze is a natural shortcut to Campfire Mind, as well as a fitting way to pass the time around the fire, if you're legal. And no liquor has quite the claim on the fire ring that whiskey has. It's whiskey we think of as the drink of choice for cowboys, prospectors, outlaws, and ladies of ill repute in the Old West. Known as "tarantula juice," "coffin varnish," and—my favorite—"neck oil," the "whiskey" sold by saloons early in the nineteenth century was a wicked brew of raw alcohol, burnt sugar, tobacco, horse apples, and whatever else happened to be at hand.

Today, bourbon, rye, scotch, Canadian whisky, and Irish whiskey are masterworks—small-batch crafted, aged in mesquite, wrapped in genuine cowhide. I prefer bourbon; the amber elixir is a rich complement to fire. The first burst of sweetness opens into smoke that spreads like a little brush fire to your belly.

I'm not sure it has to be said, but the proper way to quaff whiskey is straight. In mining camps, men who added water to whiskey may as well have worn dresses. Around the fire, whiskey circulates in a communal bottle or flask. It's neighborly, low maintenance, and as safe as sharing mouthwash. (Don't ask me how safe that is, but if mouthwash promises to kill bacteria at 40 proof, whiskey should go one better at more than twice that.) Greenhorns might add a shot of whiskey to coffee or hot chocolate for a more user-friendly jolt. One final note: The idea is not to become soused—too much of a good thing leads well past Campfire Mind to Bonfire Mind.

Whittle

Forgotten like the lost art of squirrel dressing, whittling is something to take up if you spend a lot of time around the fire. Working wood with a penknife is the hallmark of low-key, virtuous people. Sheriff Andy Taylor whittled. So does former President Jimmy Carter.

The fireside is an ideal workshop. You can just sweep up your shavings and drop them directly into the flames—along with your first mutant efforts at greatness.

For the novice, an ideal starting project is a fuzz stick. A fundamental woodworking technique for creating rooster tails, trees, and other flourishes, fuzz sticks have the other distinct advantage of burning well.

How to Create a Fuzz Stick

1. Take a piece of soft wood, about the size of a fat banana, from your kindling pile. Hold the top of the stick with one hand and brace it against a sturdy object such as a stone, a flowerpot, or the leg of a bench. (It helps if the bottom of your stick is flat and easy to keep upright.)

2. Using a penknife, cut a long, thin shaving from the top to nearly the bottom. Because you want the shavings to curl, avoid short, thick cuts. Draw your blade out so the shaving stays attached to the wood.

3. Turn the stick and repeat the process around and around until you have lots of shavings and your fuzz stick looks like a pinecone on steroids.

4. Next time you build a fire, prop your fuzz sticks upright among the kindling. Because carving to the center of the branch exposes the resin at the core, fuzz sticks make excellent firestarters.

Smoke

There was a time when sharing a pipe was an ultimate gesture of goodwill. (In some cases involving dancing bears and tie-dye, it still is.) While the health consequences of regular tobacco-use have pretty much damned the future of the pipe as an envoy of peace, an open fire pit, where clouds of carbon monoxide wax hither and thither, may be one of the last places smokers, nonsmokers, and ex-smokers can gather without a battle. After all, what is a fireplace but a giant ash tray?

That said, there are plenty of folks who object to smoking for legitimate reasons. If it's not your fireplace, ask the host or hostess before lighting up. My general feeling is that most mass-produced cigarettes stink, and, worse, they have associations with lung disease and cancer that you want to avoid in pursuit of Campfire Mind.

Somehow, against all logic, cigars and pipes rise above the fray. Hand-rolled Cubanos and meerschaum pipes conjure images of expansiveness and leisure—men in tweeds kicking back in plush leather armchairs, free from worldly concerns. Appropriately, pipes and cigars are slow-burning and require stoking and tending like the fire itself.

Things get funky when chewing tobacco enters the picture. That's strictly backwoods. The only thing more repulsive than a flying missile of chaw bursting with a loud sizzle in the middle of the fire, is when it misses.

Whatever your poison (and it is poison, of course), there is only one way to light your smoke. Plunge a stick in the coals and light your cigar, pipe, or cigarette from the flaming brand.

SIT RIGHT:

Cro-Magnon man may have perched on rocks, but we don't have to do that sort of thing. Even in the backcountry, hikers have loungers. Nothing ruins a great outdoor fire scene faster than sub-par seating. Everyone needs a clear view of the flames (this is easiest with an open pit). Chairs or benches should be supportive and snug without undermining any rustic outdoor aesthetic.

Moon Gaze

One of the major bennies of backyard fireplaces is they keep us outside after dark, providing motive and opportunity to kick back and ponder the ceiling of the world. It's true that in well-lit cities, the night sky doesn't give up its choicest fruits to stargazers. But, for all the kvetching about the millions of unseeable constellations, a choice plum hangs in our skies—bright, mysterious, and underappreciated—Missus Moon.

How to Moon Gaze

1. Buy a moon map, photographic atlas, or moon observer guide—any one of which will make you wonder why it's taken you so long to pay attention to the big cheese.

2. You can see plenty on the lunar surface with the naked eye, but scare up binoculars or a small telescope to reveal a bounty of intriguing features.

3. Moon gaze whenever you and the moon are out together. Each phase casts light and shadow in ways that reveal different characteristics on the surface. For example, when the moon is only a slim crescent, the unilluminated portion is sometimes bathed in earthshine, caused by sunlight reflected by Earth. This effect is described as "the old moon in the new moon's arms." Dark areas—lava plains called *mare*—show up well under these circumstances. As the moon waxes, you'll be able to perceive craters, peaks, mountain chains, wrinkled ridges, and the Mare Tranquillitatis (Sea of Tranquillity), where Neil Armstrong was the first person to walk on the moon in 1969.

4. One of the best ways to become familiar with the lunar surface is to sketch it. Use a pencil with an eraser and begin by drawing the big features first. Draw what you see, and don't check your guide until you're finished. The act of drawing what you see trains the eye to pick up new details. Record the date, time, and any sort of visual aid you used.

Stoke

Playing in the flames—blowing, poking, feeding—is what everyone does around a campfire. It's one of the few acceptable outlets for those of us with pyromania or attention-deficit disorder, or both. Like a well-loved guinea pig, fires thrive under a tender's dedicated attentions. Unfortunately, restraint is key—not exactly a quality for which fidgety fire-lovers are known.

So we'll keep the parameters simple.

1. Stop piling on wood. If you don't, you'll have a rager the fireplace can't contain.

2. Stop that incessant stoking. The swarms of red-hot sparks may be fun to watch but think of them as itty-bitty flying lawsuits.

3. Stop that constant stirring. Eventually, you'll snuff out your coals, creating big gusts of smoke.

DAY-AFTER TOOLS:
A shovel, a hearth broom, and an ash can make cleanup easy.

Assuming you are prepared to love your fire in a measured fashion, nothing suits this purpose better than a long, green sapling. A poker that catches on fire: What could be more to the point? If you take good care of your yard, you won't have your natural poker when you need it. So, next time you mow or rake, retrieve any long, skinny sticks and keep them near the fireplace.

Tongs, straight from the kitchen, work great when burning coal or small-cut pieces of gourmet wood. With cooking tongs you have excellent control. If you're dealing with bonfire-size logs, cast iron fire tools are the way to go. In the U.K., compulsive fire stokers rely on a lovely hand-forged steel tool called a Norfolk Fire Pipe or Fire Blower that looks like a pitchfork with curlicue tines.

Gloves are probably unnecessary unless you are cooking over the fire and handling grills and Dutch ovens. That said, they come in such elegant and rugged styles (including a twenty-inch red-leather pair that I covet) they are hard to resist. Finally, there are bellows. I'm going to go out on a limb and say if you have a pair of intact lungs you don't need bellows.

Play

For every fire zombie who is happy to nurse the Jim Beam and blob out in front of the fire, there is someone who thinks it's time for group activities. They can't help it. They are type A people, and while they shouldn't be encouraged, sometimes they must be indulged. So we all need a few easy campfire games in our back pocket.

Elvis Lives: This game has been around since long before Elvis, when it probably had a different name. Here's how you play: Light a piece of kindling in the fire until the tip has a glowing ember. Then pass the kindling around the circle. Each person blows on the ember. If it glows, the blower says, "Elvis lives," and passes the stick. Whoever holds the stick when the ember goes out loses, and has to pay a penalty in the form of another archetypal campfire tradition, Truth or Dare, wherein the loser chooses either to answer a question honestly or to perform a dare.

Wink Murder: You need at least four people for this game. More is better. To play, tear up blank scraps of paper, one for each player. On all but one scrap, write the letter V (for victim). On the last, write the letter M (for murderer). Fold up all the pieces of paper and mix them in a bowl. Each player selects a piece of paper and looks at it without showing the other players. Whoever picks the M must "kill" the other players without being caught. Murder is committed by winking at a victim, who must see the wink. When this happens, he or she pretends to die. A subtle moan and drooping head are fine, but feel free to enact the most elaborate death throes. If the murderer is caught winking by an innocent bystander, the murderer loses. The murderer wins if he or she is not found out and only one victim remains.

Liar, Liar, Pants on Fire: This simple game breaks the ice among new acquaintances and stirs up trouble among old friends. Here's how you play: A member of the group makes three statements about herself. Two must be true, while the third is false. For example, a player might say: "I know how to tap dance. I had a nose job. I studied advanced physics." (When, in truth, she can't tap.) Each of the other members of the group guesses which of the statements is false. Then the "liar" reveals the truth. For every wrong guess, the liar gets one point. For every accurate guess, the guesser gets one point. Then the next person in the circle makes three statements and the game continues. The first player to reach a predetermined number is the winner.

Follow the Bandleader: This game is a noisy version of I Packed My Grandmother's Trunk, where players string together a series of sounds. For example, the first bandleader might say, "I'm the bandleader and my song goes like this." Then she'll stamp both her feet on the ground with two stomps. The next says, "I'm the bandleader and my song goes like this." Then he stomps his feet like the first band-leader and hoots like an owl. The next might stomp her feet twice, hoot, and yodel. The next might stomp twice, hoot, yodel, and snap her fingers. You drop out of the game when you can't remember a sound in the series.

The winner is the last bandleader to perform the entire composition successfully.

Charades, Telephone, and tongue twisters are also amusing around the campfire, and pretty much all games that go over well in a car, such as Twenty Questions, work well around the fire. The License Plate Game not so well. The salient point is to avoid games with lots of props or complicated rules. Minimum effort is the overriding principle for maintaining Campfire Mind.

> **UNPLUG:**
>
> **The campfire ethos is powered down. There's enough ambient light in most neighborhoods to read by; deck lights other than candles and lanterns only detract from the main event. Stereos are out of place. The sounds around the fire are au naturel as much as possible—crackling wood, talking, laughing, singing, maybe someone plucking guitar strings.**

Drum

Your neighbors are going to be bummed if you decide to turn your backyard ring into the center of a weekly drum circle, but once in a while banging drums by firelight is a primitive gestalt that's hard to beat.

Every house should have a drum (along with a fire extinguisher and a fresh bag of Oreos), but if you don't, all kinds of household objects can be drafted into service for a makeshift jam. Tupperware bowls and empty watercooler bottles have a groovy, low resonance. Wrap fabric around the end of a wooden spoon and fasten it with string or a rubber band to make a mallet. Bottles of vitamins or aspirin, or dry beans in a water bottle, make decent maracas. Spoons are the hillbilly castanets. Don't overlook your hands and feet in helping to create a beat. Even the human voice is a percussion instrument—à la Bobby McFerrin.

If you want to get fancy without leaving home, follow the example of millions of second-graders.

How to Make a Steel Drum

1. Rinse out and dry an old tin can from coffee, tomatoes, peaches—anything, really, but the bigger the better.

2. With a marker, draw a line across the diameter of the bottom of the can. The line should be slightly off-center.

3. Take a hammer and bang the length of the line. The pitch will change as the metal stretches. Don't hammer too hard or you'll punch through the metal. You need at least two different pitches; larger cans will allow for more.

4. The eraser end of an unsharpened pencil makes an excellent drumstick.

Keep in mind that drum circles aren't about abandon. There is a balance between order and spontaneity. The whole point is to find a groove that's funky and relaxed like Campfire Mind.

Celebrate

Once you have a backyard fireplace, any day is a good day for a burn, and yet some are even better than others. Consider adding your flame to holidays in which fire has played a long and venerable role.

May Day: Along with maypoles, hilltop bonfires set by Druids were a crowning feature during ancient May Day (May 1) celebrations. The old pagan fertility festival—also known as Beltane, which means, in part, fire—was designed to bring fortune, good health, and prosperity to villages across the British Isles.

In Scotland, every household fire was extinguished on May Day and great communal fires were built according to ritual, including burning the wood of nine sacred trees. People from the community would converge on the bonfire, light brands, and swirl them in circles in honor of the sun. When the bonfire burned down, members of each household would claim some embers and use them to rekindle the home hearth.

According to tradition, leaping over a May Day fire yields good husbands for single girls, easy births for pregnant women, and health and luck for the rest of us.

Midsummer's Day: Another big fire day is midsummer's day or the summer solstice (June 20 or 21). The longest day of the year has its equivalent celebration in probably every culture. Ancient Germanic, Slav, and Celtic tribes celebrated the solstice with bonfires. The term *bonfire* comes from "bone fire," when animal bones were burned to ward off evil spirits during summer festivals. In part, the fires were burned as sympathetic magic—an earthbound jump for the sun's power. As with May Day, the fire was seen as a blessing on humans and animals, which leads to all sorts of plans for leaping and circling and so on.

Solstice was also seen as a time when fairies were abroad—as in Shakespeare's *A Midsummer Night's Dream*. Because fairies apparently can't make their own fires, they would take the embers from midsummer bonfires back to their fairy cities.

Halloween: October 31 is a natural for fire because of its spooky pedigree. But there is actually a more compelling connection. Again, we turn to the ancient Celts, who, if they were around today, would be big outdoor fireplace people. Back in the day, Celts celebrated the harvest with a bonfire, on which they would burn food as an offering to the deities. Young-

sters were charged with going through the village to collect kindling and wood for fire, and there is some belief this door-to-door collection is the basis for trick-or-treating.

Folks with portable fire pits should try moving them into the front yard on Halloween, as a neighborhood way station. On a chilly night, a lively fire can be a welcome warming spot for traveling hordes of costumed children and their chaperones.

Winter Solstice and Christmas: Burning a fire on the shortest day of the year (December 21 or 22) is a fitting way to mark the winter solstice, especially in the northern states, where the days boil down to so few hours of sunlight. Burning a tree, releasing all the energy of the sun stored through photosynthesis, is a reminder that longer, brighter days will return. Some people cut, stack, and season their Christmas tree in January to burn on the next solstice or Christmas as a symbol of renewal.

CHAPTER 4

Fire Appreciation 101

All is fire.
—Heraclitus

Fire Talk

There was a time when the crow was a very different bird than the one you see today. According to one Native American legend, she had rainbow-colored feathers and a song so sublime it made the lark close her beak. But that was long ago, before Grandfather asked one of the animals to bring the gift of fire to people, who still shivered in caves. The only creature willing to help men and women out of darkness was the crow. She took fire from the sun and flew to earth with a flaming brand in her mouth. It was a long journey for which she paid a heavy price. Over the days, the smoke scorched her throat and destroyed her voice. The flames burned her feathers black. For this great sacrifice, Grandfather gave the crow the ability to pop the tops off garbage cans.

OK, I made that last part up. But legends are flexible. This story has many versions, as do countless other tales about how we came to possess fire. A fox steals it from fireflies. A praying mantis fools an ostrich into revealing fire hidden under her wing. The mischievous Prometheus takes it from Zeus (for which he is shackled to a rock, where his liver is eaten by an eagle every day for thirteen generations, and woman is unleashed on man). But I love the notion of the lowly crow as our civilizer. It just seems right.

It's easy to be blasé about fire, especially if you're not a volcanologist or a glassblower. We dethroned its gods, deciphered its myths, and plumbed its chemical composition until it became possible to overlook fire's mojo. So with weekend firebugs in mind, we take a moment to consider our subject from the point of view of those for whom fire was a knee-trembling mystery and the stuff of religion, poetry, magic, alchemy, and eventually modern chemistry.

Drawing history and lore to the surface enriches evenings around the chimenea. Remember how discovering Van Gogh cut off his own ear made *Starry Night* a more intriguing painting? That's the idea. Like an episode of *Behind the Music*, let the story behind fire add nuance to your next weenie roast.

Myths: Gods Behaving Badly

Well before Enlightenment myth-busters translated fire into a chemical reaction, it was the purview of poets and shamans to explain the phenomenon in human terms. They described fire's capacity to transform and destroy through the lives of the gods. Their legends and myths, though thousands of years old, capture the spark of fire in a way oxygen + fuel + heat simply can't.

Probably every ancient culture and tribe that worshipped divine beings honored at least one fire/sun god, usually several if they had much experience with volcanic eruptions and wildfires. Hundreds of greater and lesser fire spirits have come down to us through time. Many are mercurial, dangerous types who need to be kept happy at all costs.

Agni, the Hindu fire god, is said to have consumed his parents when he was born, in the way fire consumes the sticks that feed it. The Chinese fire god Zhu Rong rides a tiger and is expert in revenge and executions. Ogoun—the Haitian voodoo god of war, fire, iron, thunderbolts, and, interestingly enough, politics—sports a machete and is fond of rum and tobacco.

Fire gods are also seen as patrons of civilization, protectors, and, when linked to the sun, life givers. In fact, most often divine flame-throwers are depicted as a potent mix of opposite extremes like fire itself (what scholars call duality and psychiatrists call bipolar), which makes them thrilling company.

Unfortunately, many fire gods have faded over time like old coals. They are forgotten by all but tour guides looking for local color. There is at least one lively exception: the temperamental Hawaiian/Polynesian goddess of fire and volcanoes, Pele.

AMPHIBIAN LORE:

People once thought salamanders could live in fire because of their bright red color.

This saucy hothead is still a big *kupuna* (ancestor) on the islands, and there are as many stories about Pele as there are sightings. According to one myth, Pele originally fancied herself a water goddess until one day, splashing around in the surf and digging holes in the sand, she hit magma. The sight of those fireworks inspired an abrupt change of passion.

As the volcano goddess, she is simultaneously a creator and a destroyer—qualities that are compelling in a goddess but difficult in a girlfriend. In one legend, she falls in love with a mortal and asks him to marry her. He refuses and reveals that he is in love with her sister. Pele goes all lava on them. She chases the lovers down the mountain, eventually frying them both alive. There's slim consolation in the fact that beautiful *naupaka* flowers grow in the soil above their graves.

Pele appears in various guises—as fire, lava, an old hag bumming cigarettes, a ravishing hitchhiker, and a white dog. If she's treated well, she showers good fortune on her benefactors. But cross her or take a pumice keepsake from her sacred mountainsides, and you'll live to regret it.

She's not nearly all bad, though. Pele loves surfing and sledding down volcano slopes. Hawaiians revere her creative powers and appreciate the extra real estate she lays down with regular flows. To this day, devotees make offerings in her honor, leaving berries, blossoms, and taro near active volcanoes.

Those of us who don't enjoy the pleasure of living on the islands can honor Pele just the same. Next time you fire up the backyard pit, spritz some gin on the flame; apparently that feisty booze is a favorite of the goddess.

How to Make a Colorful Offering to the Spirits of Your Choice

For millennia, mortals have tried to appease gods through elaborate rites of sacrifice. Many of these rituals included fire—incense for the Buddha, bulls for Zeus, virgins for the volcano gods.

While many rites are centered on a gift that is sacrificed, sometimes the flames themselves are an offering. Giant harvest bonfires, for example, are about the roaring spectacle. Smaller fires can also be made worthy of the gods with special woods, aromatic plants, and colored flame—either to appease an actual god, such as Verbti (the ancient Albanian blind fire deity who couldn't abide foul mouths), or to impress the guy with the divine biceps next door.

Break out of the old ruby flame rut. Stores that carry fireplace accessories often sell flame colorants in a crystal form that you can sprinkle directly on the fire to create a rainbow effect. Or try a homespun option: Several ingredients in cooking, laundry, and cleaning supplies react with fire to produce colored flames. But sprinkling Borax or table salt directly into your fire—and potentially allowing it to waft into someone's eyes—isn't the best way to spin the color wheel. Try an attractive intermediary like the lovely pinecone.

1. Take a dozen or so dry pinecones and soak them in a solution of one pound table salt or Borax or Epsom salt (see step 2) and one gallon of water for twenty-four hours.

2. Choose your magic powder. Different solutions yield different results. For example, magnesium sulfate, the active ingredient in Epsom salt, turns flames white. Borax makes flames yellowish-green. Sodium chloride (or table salt) creates a yellow flame. Potassium chloride, which is used as a salt substitute, is a purple colorant. Copper sulfate, which is used in pools, turns fire and sometimes swimmers' hair green.

3. After they're done soaking, remove the pinecones from the mixture and set them on a towel to dry.

4. Once dry, they are ready to toss into a burning fire. A mix of pinecones soaked in different solutions will create a mix of colors. Some folks soak sawdust, cork, or even whole logs for color effects.

A word of warning: Don't use colorants if you plan to roast hot dogs or marshmallows or cook anything whatsoever. Some of these chemicals will create a fairly toxic barbecue.

Philosophy: Red Hot Building Block

In the eons between the end of subsistence living and the invention of the Gameboy, people spent some of their free time trying to explain how the world was made. And very early on, these explanations divided the universe into a handful of basic ingredients. From Han dynasty China to Elizabethan England, gurus, philosophers, and alchemists identified a few fundamental elements. They all included fire.

Ancient Greek philosophers maintained that the universe was comprised of air, earth, water, and fire—with the occasional addition of a fifth, heavenly or eternal element. Among these, fire was endowed with special powers. The Stoics, for example, believed it held the world together. These classical categories were so compelling a model of the world that they persisted well into the Middle Ages and the Renaissance.

But the Greeks were by no means the first. Centuries before Plato dialogued with Aristotle, the Chinese were dividing the world into five phases. Metal, wood, water, fire, and earth are woven into the I Ching, Chinese cosmology, astrology, and feng shui, the philosophy-turned-fad. The Chinese phases are active and interrelated. So, for example, fire is generated by wood and, in turn, generates earth. Fire is destroyed by water and, in turn, destroys metal.

More than 5,000 years ago on the Indian subcontinent, Hindu swamis claimed nature

CLASSIC CREMATION:

According to legend, the ancient Greek philosopher Empedocles, who believed fire was one of a few basic elements making up the universe, threw himself into the Mount Etna volcano, leaving his Tevas behind on the crater's edge.

and humans comprised five fundamental principles. Taken together as the Panchabhootha, these include Bhoomi (earth), Jala (water), Vayu (air), Agni (fire), and Akasa (space). Agni, the patricidal god of fire mentioned earlier, was seen as the mediator between heaven and earth for his role in consuming sacrifices.

The critical feature of all these schemes is balance. Keeping the elements or phases or principles in proper equilibrium ensures good health, prosperity, and all the yummy stuff in between. Hippocrates, the father of the television hospital drama, believed that disease resulted from an imbalance of the four bodily humors, which were essentially the four elements—yellow bile (water), black bile (earth), blood (fire), and phlegm (air). While it made for great poetic imagery, it didn't lead to the best health care. Hindus had better luck integrating their five principles into the long-lasting Ayurvedic tradition.

Feng shui is also all about balance, as anyone who has picked up a home design magazine in the past ten years can tell you. According to the principles of feng shui, integrating (aka decorating with) metal, wood, water, fire, and earth, according to certain prescriptions, enhances the flow of chi (energy).

Good chi flow contributes to beauty, harmony, and tranquillity.

Today, we may not think in terms of elements, but the notion of striving for balance is commonplace. Like the ancients, we see balance as a key to the good life. Although we experience plenty of air, earth, and water in the regular course of a day, we can go weeks without a good dose of fire. More exposure to real flame will invigorate and balance the elements in our lives.

How to Foster Long Life and Happiness with a Backyard Fireplace

1. Stand in the center of your garden.

2. Face south. If you're not certain which way is south, I'd suggest using a compass. (But if you can't point south, you probably don't know how to use a compass. Haul out a city map to orient yourself.) The crucial point is that in feng shui, south represents opportunity, achievement, happiness, and longevity. It is also the domain of fire, which means this is where you put your fire pit or even a barbecue grill.

3. Clear away any water elements. As you might expect, this is not the place for your water fountain, pond, or hose. They belong in the north.

4. If you want plantings anywhere near your fireplace, red flowers and pointy-shaped plants are best in the south, because they are associated with the color and tapered tips of flame.

There is much more to feng shui, including the other phases and directions that need to be properly addressed. But fire is a powerful place to begin.

One caveat has to be offered. Followers of Agni (associated with sex and virility in men, by the way) face fires in different directions for different purposes. East-facing fires are for sacrifices to the gods; south-facing are for sacrifices to the spirits of the dead; west-facing are for cooking.

Quest for Plasma

You can't keep a good idea down. While it's easy to treat the elements as a poetic notion, today chemists pretty much define the world along similar lines. The modern-day "states of matter" are solid, liquid, gas, and something called *plasma*. Plasma is an ionized gas that is electronically conductive. That's pretty much the textbook definition, because I wouldn't know plasma if someone used it to light my cigar. What matters is that the properties of plasma are different from the three ordinary states of matter. Thus, it is considered a distinct state, and the four elements endure. (That said, Earth, Wind and Fire make some pretty righteous funk with only three.)

Chemistry: Combustion Junction

Because of its constantly moving, changing nature, fire is almost as painful to define as it is to touch. For more than a million years of cohabitating with this superheated element, we never really got close to comprehending its chemical nature. The first meaningful stab was in the seventeenth century, when two German chemists developed a theory of flammability. Their idea was that certain materials contained an odorless, colorless, tasteless, and weightless flammable essence, which they dubbed *phlogiston*. When something was burned, according to the theory, it was said to be "dephlogisticated," as in, "I can't eat *this*. This steak is dephlogisticated!"

Of course, most of us never learned about phlogiston because in the decades before the French Revolution, two other European scientists pitched the theory into the rubbish heap and launched modern chemistry. The first was a cantankerous Englishman named Joseph Priestley, who determined that air was not an elementary substance, but rather it was composed of more basic components including oxygen. In conversations and correspondence with a well-born overachiever named Antoine-Laurent de Lavoisier, Priestley pointed out that mice were more chipper and candles burned more brightly in oxygenated environments.

Lavoisier was off and running. He capitalized on Priestley's beginnings and made the critical determination that oxygen, not phlogiston, is the key to combustion. He also laid out the system of modern elements for the first time.

Unfortunately, brilliance was no defense during the Reign of Terror, when all noblemen (especially a wealthy tax collector like Lavoisier) were deemed traitors. In 1794, the father of modern chemistry was tried, convicted, and guillotined in one day.

Despite his remarkable breakthrough in understanding combustion, Lavoisier is often remembered for an apocryphal story surrounding his execution. (I mention it here not because I prefer bizarre gossip to high-minded science but because it's a good fireside anecdote.) The story goes that Lavoisier was so compulsively curious that he turned his final breaths into an experiment to determine how long a severed head maintained consciousness. He planned to blink as many times as possible *after* he lost his head. His unlucky assistant was to observe and count. According to the legend, he blinked more than a dozen times.

Two hundred years later, biologists say Lavoisier couldn't have consciously blinked even once, but oxygen remains at the heart of the chemistry of combustion. As it is understood today, fire is the combination of oxygen and fuel in the presence of heat, typically characterized by flame, which is incandescent gas that contains and sustains the reaction and emits light and heat. (That exacting definition comes by way of "The Straight Dope" columnist Cecil Adams.)

Space Fire

In micro- or zero-G environments, fire looks different than here on Earth. During a romantic dinner on the international space station, for instance, a candle flame wouldn't be pointy but spherical. That's because gravity determines the shape of flame. On Earth, gases in a flame are less dense than surrounding air, so they move upward toward lower pressure. It's why flames *climb* tree trunks and drapes. Also, because there is no oxygen in space, astronauts have to carry their own supply not just for breathing but to fire up rocket engines for the trip home.

The Moth Quandary

Moths drawn inexorably toward fire is one of the enduring romantic clichés of our time. While our left brains are engaged, let's explore the science.

For a long time, it was believed that these nocturnal critters made their way in the world with an internal light compass, using the distant moon as a beacon. The popular theory was that when moths were close to a flame, it threw off the compass and caused them to circle the flickering light in ever-smaller rotations until they met their moth-maker.

But an enterprising entomologist demonstrated that moths fly in a straight line toward a flame until they get close, and then swerve off and circle the light at a cautious distance—rarely getting burned—until, eventually, they flitter off to a safe, dark corner, like your sweater drawer.

On the other hand, mosquitoes (especially females) *are* definitely attracted to fire—ctually to heat, carbon dioxide, and carbon monoxide. That's because warm-blooded humans exhale carbon dioxide, which acts like a neon "all you can eat" sign. On top of this, most mosquitoes feed after dark—fire time—or early morning. So, in your next sonnet, remember the fair mosquito drawn to the flame, and if you live in New Jersey, on the Mosquito Coast, or in other bug-happy regions, consider burning piñon pine firewood or citronella candles to keep bloodsuckers at bay.

How to Create a Fire Extinguisher... Sort of

This is a classic kid-science experiment, the kind of thing the Beave might try alone in his bedroom and end up setting the entire house on fire. (There's a warning there.) It's also easy science you can perform with typical household ingredients that illustrates some of the principles of fire chemistry and the real value of the fire extinguisher you bought along with your fire kettle.

Fire extinguishers don't douse fire with water. If they did, they'd have to be a whole lot bigger. Instead, they work by removing the critical ingredient of oxygen from the immediate atmosphere. Here's another way to observe the process without the mess of the real thing.

1. Place a cereal bowl upright inside a larger, deep bowl.

2. Fill the smaller bowl with about a third of a cup of baking soda.

3. Upright in the baking soda, place a short candle (such as a votive or birthday candle, about two inches tall) and a slightly taller candle (a three-inch candle stub works well). Make sure they are secure in the soda.

4. Light the candles.

5. Carefully, pour vinegar into the bowl of baking soda, taking care to avoid the candles.

When vinegar is combined with baking soda, they react to produce carbon dioxide, which, when it reaches the flame, replaces oxygen in the immediate vicinity and snuffs the fire. Since CO_2 is heavier than the surrounding air, it sinks to the bottom of the bowl. But as the reaction continues and carbon dioxide builds up, the bowl fills with the heavier gas and rises to the level of the candle flame, which is why the taller candle goes out after the shorter one.

CHAPTER 5

Ghost Stories and Sing-alongs

On top of spaghetti, all covered with cheese,
I lost my poor meatball, when somebody sneezed.
—Tom Glazer

Campfire Culture

In *Star Trek V: The Final Frontier*, Dr. McCoy, Spock, and Captain Kirk take shore leave together at Yosemite National Park, which looks in the twenty-third century remarkably like it does in the twenty-first. After a day of McCoy complaining, Spock darting around in jet boots, and Kirk solo-climbing El Capitán, the old friends gather around a campfire.

McCoy spoons beans from a Dutch oven and shares a fifth of whiskey with Kirk as they reminisce about camping days of yore. Meanwhile, Spock doesn't quite get the campfire scene but being the universe's biggest nerd, he has come prepared. Before the holiday, he researched camping customs on the ship's computer. Flashing his newfound knowledge, Spock

proudly produces a marshmallow from a gizmo that looks like a flashlight and declares he is ready to toast. He's stiff and formal, even when his friends try to coax him into singing rounds of "Row, Row, Row Your Boat."

It's vintage Star Trek—the future men in their space-age leisure wear acting like cowboys to the eternal mystification of their half-Vulcan buddy. From our perspective, the salient plot detail is the idea that if Spock were to research campfires on a state-of-the-art computer 200 years in the future, he'd discover marshmallows. Who can doubt it?

There is a long history of habit and ritual that comes into play when we gather around a campfire, from Lascaux 15000 BCE to Yosemite 2200 CE. Certain habits—such as repairing snares and braiding rope—have fallen off, especially around urban fire pits, but roasting marshmallows, singing, and storytelling are still going strong.

Goblins, Spooks, and Shades, Oh My!

Fire rings through the ages have hosted every imaginable story—from legends, histories, and fables to fish stories, jokes, and stinging gossip. But of all the stories shared around a fire, spooky yarns are the urtext. There is something in the human genetic code that makes us relish having the bejesus scared out of us.

Sure, hair-raising tales can be told in other settings. A warm bed in a darkened room is a decent second choice, but it has nothing over a fire out-of-doors. First of all, flames often factor into scary stories. Witches are burned at the stake. Haunted houses spontaneously combust. Vampires can be destroyed by fire. (Although for any newbie slayers out there, I should point out that the vampire has to be burned entirely to ashes or he will somehow pull himself back together and wreak some heavy vengeance.)

Second, flames provide deliciously creepy atmospherics. There is the ghastly light in the faces of your unnerved companions. Unpredictable pops and flares keep everyone on edge. Dancing shadows transform a garden hose into a nameless menace. And while the fire keeps our hands and faces warm, our backs are exposed and maybe coolish—ripe for goose bumps.

Nine Storytelling Tips and Six Starter Tales

It takes more than a poltergeist to make a ghost story. There's an art to putting it over. So here's some expert advice and a few starter stories to help would-be yarn spinners. Many of these techniques come from Stuart Stotts, a musician and writer in Madison, Wisconsin, who has been a full-time storyteller for almost two decades. In his experience, audiences never fail to request at least one ghost story. We like to be unsettled, Stotts says. But it takes practice to unsettle just right.

1. Know your audience. Young children are easily frightened. Some adults are, too, but that's their problem. Stotts draws the line at about seven years old for real ghost stories. He also knows that younger audiences enjoy "the jump"—the surprise moment that makes them scream. (See tip 8 for details.)

Middle school students have an appetite for gore. So, if your story has a slasher or a serial killer, you're probably in good shape. Stotts doesn't dabble in violence. When he tells stories to middle school kids, they'll listen edgy and rapt but when it's over, they'll say, "That wasn't a ghost story. There wasn't any blood."

Adults generally don't like the violence; they prefer mystery and suspense. They like to be surprised but not duped. They also like stories with local settings and history, which brings us to tip 2.

2. Make it immediate. There are two ways to accomplish this. Talk about weird events you or people you've known experienced directly, or lay claim to an old favorite. Be the eyewitness to weirdness.

For example, the "Vanishing Hitchhiker" is an oldie but a goodie told a hundred different ways, even immortalized in country western songs. It's a great tale for spicing up with local details such as a roadside stop that's well-known to your audience. "You know that ice cream stand near Avon, where we blew out a tire last year? Well, a friend of mine picked up a hitchhiker there last week. . . ." See how that works? Here's a version of the story told as if it happened to me and my sister just the other day.

My sister Whitney and I were driving home last Sunday after a weekend in the mountains. We left pretty late to avoid traffic, and it must have been nearly midnight by the time we reached the city outskirts. We stopped to get gas, and as we drove up the highway on-ramp, Whitney shouted, "Stop!"

"What the heck?" I asked. I slowed and eased onto the shoulder. Then, I saw the girl in my rearview mirror. She looked only about thirteen. She was hitchhiking!

Whitney called out to her. "Where you headed?"

"I live in Seattle," she said.

Whitney told her to hop in.

We asked her where home was, and it turned out to be only about a mile from my place, so we decided to deliver her to her front stoop. Even if it had been a hundred miles from my house, we would have taken her all the way.

I had a million questions, first among them why a young girl would be out on the roadside hitchhiking at this cold and dark hour wearing nothing but a T-shirt and jeans. She looked completely chilled. Her face was white and her lips purple.

It was warm in the car, but Whitney asked the hitchhiker if she'd like to wear her coat, which was on the back seat next to the girl. She said thanks, and wrapped the big wool jacket around her. Before I could ask her name, I saw that the hitchhiker was asleep.

When we reached her house, she woke up instantly. We started to get out of the car to walk her to the front door and have a word with her mom or dad, but she stopped us. She said, "Thank you. I'm fine." Then she sprinted toward the back of the house. It

didn't seem right to follow her. I don't know why.

It wasn't until the next morning, as we got ready to walk my dog, that we realized the girl had run off with Whitney's coat. So that afternoon, we went back to the house to ask for the coat. It was a good excuse to be sure the girl was all right.

A grizzled old man, who looked too old to be the hitchhiker's father, answered the door. He looked tough, mean even. And I noticed he had a blue tooth. I was nervous, for the girl's sake and our own. But Whitney jumped in and described the events of the previous night.

"You say she looked about thirteen?" the man asked. "Did she have long black hair? Was she wearing a white T-shirt and blue jeans?"

"Yes. Yes," Whitney and I said in unison.

"Well, folks, you're not the first," he said. Then he paused. I tried looking past him into the hallway for any sign of the girl. "You see . . ." And he paused again. He had this funny look, like he wasn't sure about *us*. "That girl's been dead for more than twenty years. She was killed in a car accident down near that very exit where you saw her hitching. Her parents used to live in this house."

We were stunned. "That can't be true," Whitney said. "I don't believe you. Where's the girl?"

"Her name's Eilleen Wescott. She's buried at Lakeside Cemetery. I suggest you go to her grave, if you don't believe me." Then he closed the door.

We just stood there for a few minutes, staring at the knocker, trying to figure out if it were true. I broke the silence.

"Let's go to the cemetery," I said.

"What will that prove? That guy is off his rocker. Or worse, he's lying," Whitney said. She wanted to call the police. I told her we could call the police, but only if we went to the cemetery first. I was curious if an Eilleen Wescott had ever existed.

The sky was already pretty dusky by the time we arrived at the cemetery. We found an attendant, who knew exactly what we were looking for. He pointed east.

We walked across the wet grass, and it seemed to become night in just the few minutes we'd been there. Then we saw it: Eilleen's tombstone. It was too dark to read the name, but we didn't have to. Heaped at the base of the stone was Whitney's wool coat.

3. Don't fall in love with the sound of your own voice. You'll be the only one. Keep ghost stories short. Five to seven minutes tops. If people ask for more, tell another one. If they don't, keep quiet.

4. If you tell more than one story—even after we said not to—vary the pace and tension. Stotts opens his ghost story performances with the song "I'm Not Scared" by folk songwriter Bob Blue. (You can find it on Stotts's recording by the same name.) The song plays on the notion of kids saying "I'm not scared" when they really are, and how they say it more loudly and more often the more frightened they become. It's lighthearted, and it relaxes listeners.

The other thing Stotts does is tell humorous ghost stories. When you sprinkle a playful ghost story in with the serious ones, people relax and let down their guard. You can pounce again later.

If you have a fairly large group gathered around the fire, add the element of participation. The story of "The Ghost of One Black Eye" is a good example. Enlist your audience to be the voice of the phantom. When you cue them, they should say in as eerie a voice as possible, "I am the ghost of one black eye." Have them practice a few times before you begin.

Here's an abbreviated version of the story, with stage directions.

A family from out of state moves into a mansion, which the parents bought at a surprisingly cut-rate price. During the first week, as everyone is emptying boxes, the father bumps into a ghost in the pantry. The horrible wraith bellows. [Cue listeners.] "I am the ghost of one black eye." The father runs screaming from the house.

Meanwhile, the mother is merrily hanging hacksaws and hammers on hooks in the workshop. Suddenly, she, too, bumps into the ghost. Again, he pours out his lamentation. [Cue listeners.] "I am the ghost of one black eye." She, like her husband before her, runs screaming from the house.

Next comes the oldest brother, who is breaking down boxes. He sees the ghost. It wails. The boy runs. And so on, until the ghost frightens nearly everyone in the family, leaving only the youngest child, a girl of about four. [If you have a youngster among your listeners, make the boy or girl in the story the same sex and age.] The girl is playing in the attic when she sees the ghost. Knowing he has almost cleared off the entire family, the specter howls in his most fearful voice. [Cue listeners.] "I am the ghost of one black eye."

The girl turns on her heels, raises her fists, and says, "Yeah. Well, if you don't be quiet and leave us alone, you're gonna be the ghost of *two* black eyes!"

5. Use sound. One of the best stories around for the crafty use of sound is "Cross-country Trip." Again, this urban legend has been told in various guises probably ever since the advent of car radios. It's essentially the story of a young couple that becomes stuck (runs out of gas, collides with a tree) in a remote location in the middle of the night. She waits with the car, while he goes to get gas (help, the hell out of there). She listens to the radio and hears about an "escaped homicidal lunatic" (or E.H.L.). Understandably, she is very, very frightened. Eventually—and the story is probably coming back to you now—she hears tap, tap, tap on the roof of the car. This tapping goes on for some time, while the traumatized girl frets about whether to get out of the car and investigate.

The source of the tapping is pretty gruesome, ideally suited for a pack of adolescent listeners. In the version I grew up with, the police arrive and try to lure the girl out of the car, telling her not to turn her head to investigate the source of the sound. Of course, she does. She sees the E.H.L. up in a tree, rapping the car roof with a stick that has her boyfriend's severed head stuck on its end—a visual that is especially keen for marshmallow roasts.

To make the sound work, you have to plan ahead. Be sure you have a stick in your hand before you begin your story. The stick should appear to be an afterthought. Then, when it's

time for the taps in the story, rap the stick against something nearby. A metal roasting fork against a cast-iron fire pit has a terrifying ring.

6. Entertain with the strange and exotic. Just as local details draw us into a story, the exotic also adds intrigue. This story is called "Diplomacy" and was written by Lafcadio Hearn around the turn of the twentieth century. It's wonderfully strange and magical, a welcome break from naive boys and girls in the dark.

It had been ordered that the execution should take place in the garden. So the man was taken

there and made to kneel down in a wide, sanded space crossed by a line of *tobi-ishi,* or stepping-stones, such as you may still see in Japanese landscape gardens. His arms were bound behind him. Retainers brought water in buckets and rice bags filled with pebbles; and they packed the rice bags round the kneeling man—so wedging him in that he could not move. The master came, and observed the arrangements. He found them satisfactory and made no remarks.

Suddenly, the condemned man cried out to him:

"Honored sir, the fault for which I have been doomed I did not wittingly commit. It was only my very great stupidity that caused the fault. Having been born stupid, by reason of my karma, I could not always help making mistakes. But to kill a man for being stupid is wrong—and that wrong will be repaid. So surely as you kill me, so surely shall I be avenged; out of the resentment that you provoke will come the vengeance; and evil will be rendered for evil."

If any person be killed while feeling strong resentment, the ghost of that person will be able to take vengeance upon the killer. This the samurai knew. He replied very gently—almost caressingly:

"We shall allow you to frighten us as much as you please—after you are dead. But it is difficult to believe that you mean what you say. Will you try to give us some sign of your great resentment—after your head has been cut off?"

"Assuredly I will," answered the man.

"Very well," said the samurai, drawing his long sword, "I am now going to cut off your head. Directly in front of you there is a stepping-stone. After your head has been cut off, try to bite the stepping-stone. If your angry ghost can help you to do that, some of us may be frightened. Will you try to bite the stone?"

"I will bite it!" cried the man, in great anger. "I will bite it! I will bite—"

There was a flash, a swish, a crunching thud: The bound body bowed over the rice sacks—two long blood-jets pumping from the shorn neck—and the head rolled upon the sand. Heavily toward the stepping-stone it rolled. Then, suddenly bounding, it caught the upper edge of the stone between its teeth, clung desperately for a moment, and dropped inert.

None spoke; but the retainers stared in horror at their master. He seemed to be quite unconcerned. He merely held out his sword to the nearest attendant, who, with a wooden dipper, poured water over the blade from haft to point, and then carefully wiped the steel several times with sheets of soft paper. And thus ended the ceremonial part of the incident.

For months thereafter, the retainers and the domestics lived in ceaseless fear of ghostly visitation. None of them doubted that the promised vengeance would come, and their constant terror caused them to hear and to see much that did not exist. They became afraid of the sound of the wind in the bamboo—afraid even of the stirring of shadows in the garden. At last, after taking counsel together, they decided to petition their master to have a *segaki* service performed on behalf of the vengeful spirit.

"Quite unnecessary," the samurai said, when his chief retainer had uttered the general wish. "I understand that the desire of a dying man for revenge may be a cause for fear. But in this case there is nothing to fear."

The retainer looked at his master beseechingly, but hesitated to ask the reason for this alarming confidence.

"Oh, the reason is simple enough," declared the samurai, divining the unspoken doubt. "Only the very last intention of that fellow could have been dangerous; and when I challenged him to give me the sign, I diverted his mind from the desire for revenge. He died with the set purpose of biting the stepping-stone, and that purpose he was able to accomplish, but nothing else. All the rest he must have forgotten. So you need not feel any further anxiety about the matter."

And indeed the dead man gave no more trouble. Nothing at all happened.

7. If the fire is roaring and the kids want a good scare, wing it. Let a local landmark such as the vine-covered shed down the street or the rope swing by the lake inspire a spontaneous story. Once your kids hear about the old man with cork toes who lived in the shed or the one-eyed banshee who tried to lure you to play, they will never look at these familiar landmarks the same way again. There is a long and noble tradition of grown-ups embroidering the truth for amusement and purpose. Some ghost stories evolve as a way to keep children away from dangerous places.

For example, the legend of "La Llorona" (The Crying Woman) is commonly told in a variety of different forms in Mexico. Its main aim was probably to scare children away from the banks of fast-flowing rivers, but it is also an allegory for the loss of the native people under Spain's conquest. Here's a short version that freely blends history and fantasy.

In 1519, the Spaniard Hernán Cortés began his conquest of Mexico by taking many captives. Among them was a wise and lonely woman, La Malinche, who fell instantly in love with the fearless conquistador. As a gift, she revealed to him how he could conquer her country. She betrayed her people for her passion, but she was so happy she did not think about it.

During Cortés's years of conquest, she lived as his wife and had three children by him. But he eventually returned to Spain to celebrate his triumph and to marry a noblewoman. La Malinche was humiliated and universally reviled. She was furious with Cortés. Out of spite, she drowned all three of their children in the river. Then, overcome by the deed, she drowned herself.

If you go near the river at night, you can hear the crying woman's voice in the water. She laments, *"Mis hijos, mis hijos, dónde están mis hijos?"* which means, "My children, my children, where are my children?"

Sometimes, La Malinche mistakes children who wander along the banks without their parents as her own and grabs them to her breast. They, too, drown.

8. Master the pause. This is perhaps the most critical and difficult refinement in telling stories of any kind, and it is especially important with scary stories. The pause is that tiny hesitation before you spring the surprise (or what Stotts calls "the jump"). You can't have one without the other. In an essay on how to tell a story, Mark Twain describes the pause this way: "It is a dainty thing, and delicate, and also uncertain and treacherous; for it must be exactly the right length—no more and no less—or it fails of its purpose and makes trouble. If the pause is too short the impressive point is passed, and

the audience have had time to divine that a surprise is intended—and then you can't surprise them."

The story both Twain and Stotts cite as an example of the pause and the jump is "The Golden Arm." There are as many versions of this classic as there are straws in a witch's broom. In one story, a boy finds a golden arm in a cemetery and keeps it in a shoebox. In this version, a woman with a golden arm is betrayed.

Once upon a time, there was a man whose wife had a golden arm. She was extremely proud of her lovely shiny biceps and triceps, her long, glowing fingers, and her dainty, yellow wrist.

One day as she was buffing her arm, she told her husband, "If I die before you, promise to bury me with my golden arm." He promised. When she died, he buried her with the golden arm right alongside her.

But after a while he began to think about the arm—all that gold six feet under, doing no one any good. He told himself that someone else in the village might dig up the grave to steal the arm. The more he thought about it, the more he was sure he should retrieve it, just to be sure no one else did. So one dark night, he went to the graveyard and dug up his wife's grave and filched the golden arm.

He tucked the valuable prosthesis under his long coat. On the way home, rain began to fall. The rain turned to hail and then snow. The wind kicked up and was blowing gale force by the time he got home. He had a sinking feeling.

He put the golden arm on the kitchen table. Then he moved it to a chair. But the arm that had always been attached to his wife's body never looked quite right without her. So, finally, he climbed into bed and put the arm under the covers with him—just like when his wife had been alive. But this night the arm was as cold as ice. It froze him to the marrow. He shivered and listened to the storm.

The winds gusted outside and the man thought he heard a cry. [At this point, switch to your most ghoulish voice and repeat a few times, first in a whisper, and then increasing in volume:]

"Who has got my golden arm? Who has got my golden arm? WHO HAS GOT MY GOLDEN ARM?" The man pulled the covers up around his ears so he wouldn't hear it. But it just kept getting louder: "WHO HAS GOT MY GOLDEN ARM?"

Then he heard it on the porch: "WHO HAS GOT MY GOLDEN ARM?"

The wind howled as the front door flew open. The man shook under the covers. The voice was coming up the stairs! "WHO HAS

GOT MY GOLDEN ARM?" Then the door to his room burst open. He peeked out from his covers. There was something there but he could see right through it.

"WHO HAS GOT MY GOLDEN ARM?"

He felt the thing breathing on him next to the bed. He'd never been so scared. He thought he'd die of fright.

"WHO HAS GOT MY GOLDEN ARM?"

He pulled the quilt up over his head.

"WHO HAS GOT MY GOLDEN ARM?"

The quilt slid from his grasp. He struggled to keep the blanket up around his head, but the voice was too strong. The man edged to the corner of the bed. He couldn't speak. The bed rattled from his shaking.

"WHO HAS GOT MY GOLDEN ARM?"

[Settle your eyes on one listener for that everything's-riding-on-it pregnant pause, and then pounce.]
"YOU'VE GOT IT!"

My husband remembers his father telling this story, especially the disconcerting way he had of swinging a big stiff arm in a wide arc until it landed on the shoulder of the most vulnerable listener. One tip with this story, or any other ghostly gotcha tale: Pick your victim in advance, and be near enough to them that you can spring your trap without giving it away beforehand.

9. Make room for the un-story. Prepared stories are always good fun, but uncrafted anecdotes and fragments are compelling, too. In his work collecting ghost stories in Wisconsin, Stotts discovered that a surprising number of people have seen or experienced or felt something they classify as a ghostly event. When the conversation turns to ghost stories, many people say, "I had something happen to *me* once." If you're lucky enough to hear those words, give up the mike.

Campfires are an ideal setting for this sort of sharing—they are a portal to the other side and can become opportunities not just for storytelling but also for discovering something new in friends and family.

Where to Find Creepy Tales

Ghost stories don't have to have a ghost per se, just something mysterious and unexplainable. Folk tales, urban legends, fragments from your childhood—anything that interests you will do. What's surprising is how many stories you know without realizing it. Of all the stories just mentioned, I'm sure a few were familiar. Plus, hearing one story around the fire has a way of triggering others you couldn't possibly have recalled in less conducive circumstances.

Another place to look is story collections. Check out *The Bookcase Ghost: A Storyteller's Collection of Wisconsin Ghost Stories* by Stotts and Elizabeth Matson. Stotts also recommends Alvin Schwartz's spooky compendiums, including *Scary Stories to Tell in the Dark*.

Kum-ba-yah Time

There isn't enough group singing anymore. If you're lucky, you enjoy a dose in school and church. Otherwise, it's a world of iPods, karaoke, and arias in the shower. And that's a loss, because when people sing together, even when the singing is not particularly high caliber, all participants are enriched by the experience. Sing in a group and you are carried along by other voices in a current—over rough spots where you can't manage the note or remember the lyric—toward a sound that is more than the sum of the individual voices. Even true divas can't experience this sort of thing on their own.

An outdoor fire creates a new and welcome space for the endangered, communal art of the sing-along. It's a reflex, really: Two people at a fire is a duet, three is a trio, and so on.

As for the repertoire, it's like with ghost stories, anyone of a certain age knows at least a dozen campfire songs. The singing part of the sing-along is only half the joy. The other bonus is rummaging around in your hippocampus, dusting off corny favorites from the past ("Streets of Laredo," "Oh! Susanna," "On Top of Old Smoky") and saddling the next generation with those silly, sappy refrains.

It's my firm belief that the best campfire songs are those that stand up well under really bad singing. That's why comic songs or songs with noises and shouts are so perfect for the fire. They don't brook American Idol–style arias or even song leaders. They build camaraderie and reward heart over talent.

That doesn't mean it's not worthwhile to take a crack at more challenging songs or even rounds. My father was always attempting to orchestrate a grand harmony of "Keep the Home Fires Burning" and "There's a Long, Long Trail." Unfortunately for him, only three of his seven children could carry a tune. I suspect it's why he married my stepmother, who loved to camp and had four daughters with fine voices.

Six Songs to Warm Up Your Voice Box

There are lots of songbooks out there. Before the Internet, we found much of this sort of thing at the library, and it's still the go-to spot for retro collections of cowboy ballads, spirituals, folk songs, sea chanteys, and patriotic anthems—all of which are well suited for sing-alongs. Second-hand bookstores are another rich source for old scouting-song compendiums and hymn books.

If that's too analog for you, there's plenty online. One of my favorite Web sites is scoutsongs.com. This is a virtual songbook created by Jonathan Glassman, a camper in the early eighties at Tanah Keeta Scout Reservation in Tequest, Florida. Later, he worked at the camp for three summers. During that time he compiled a songbook, which he preserved online in 2002. Since then, he has added other camp songs and included Girl Scout–specific songs with the help of his mother and sister.

Scoutsongs.com includes lyrics and, especially helpful, musical accompaniment for more than a hundred standards. If you can't remember the tune to a song not listed on Glassman's site, try a general search. Music files for many standards are available on the Internet.

I suspect you won't need more than a little prompting. So here are some classic (by no means all classy) campfire songs to grease the cogs. Sing a few of these and the floodgates of bad taste and sentimentality will surely open.

Found a Peanut
This is sung to the tune of "Clementine" and really has no definitive version. Feel free to ad-lib.

> *1.*
> *Found a peanut,*
> *found a peanut,*
> *found a peanut just now.*
> *Just now I found a peanut,*
> *found a peanut just now.*

2.

It was rotten,
it was rotten,
it was rotten just now.
Just now it was rotten,
it was rotten just now.

3. *Ate it anyway. . .*
4. *Got real sick. . .*
5. *Called the doctor. . .*
6. *Had to have surgery. . .*
7. *Died anyway. . .*
8. *Went to heaven. . .*
9. *Kicked St. Peter. . .*
10. *Went the other way. . .*
11. *Found a peanut. . .*
12. *Threw it away. . .*

Shoo, Fly, Don't Bother Me

I like a good nonsense song. There's a long tradition of lyrics where the point is a big mystery—from "John Jacob Jingleheimer Schmidt" to "Jimmy Crack Corn." In the case of "Shoo, Fly," what's all that morning star business about?

Shoo, fly, don't bother me,
Shoo, fly, don't bother me,
Shoo, fly, don't bother me,
For I belong to somebody.

I feel, I feel,
I feel like a morning star,
I feel, I feel,
I feel like a morning star.

She'll Be Comin' Round the Mountain

Songs that allow you to get raucous and loud are a definite boon around an urban campfire. "She'll Be Comin' Round the Mountain" has the added challenge of a memory element. Don't be limited by these mere eight verses. Create your own.

1.
She'll be comin' round the mountain,
when she comes. Toot, toot!
She'll be comin' round the mountain,
when she comes. Toot, toot!
She'll be comin' round the mountain
She'll be comin' round the mountain
She'll be comin' round the mountain
when she comes. Toot, toot!

2.
She'll be driving six white horses, when
she comes. Whoa, there!
She'll be driving six white horses, when
she comes. Whoa, there!
She'll be driving six white horses.
She'll be driving six white horses.
She'll be driving six white horses, when
she comes. Whoa, there! Toot, toot!

3.
Oh, we'll all go out to meet her, when
she comes. Hiya babe!
Oh, we'll all go out to meet her, when
she comes. Hiya babe!
Oh, we'll all go out to meet her.
We'll all go out to meet her.
We'll all go out to meet her, when she
comes.
Hiya babe! Whoa, there! Toot, toot!

4. *She'll be wearing silk pajamas, when*
she comes. (wolf whistle)
5. *And, we'll wear our bright red woolies,*
when she comes. Scratch, scratch!
6. *Oh, we'll all have chicken and*
dumplings, when she comes. Yum, yum!
(or yuck, yuck!)
7. *Oh, we'll all have indigestion, when she*
comes. Burp, burp!
8. *She will have to sleep with grandma,*
when she comes. (Snoring sound.)

Home on the Range

You have to have at least one rootin' tootin' cowboy song in your repertoire, a cowpoke's paean to the desert, a dancing gal, or a velvety steer. Go for something slow and rhythmic that could be sung easily while you sway in the saddle (and might even inspire a discreet yodel). Of course, the saddle is purely a metaphor. I like "Home on the Range," a traditional work with many variations that serves our purposes nicely, without raising questions about your relationship with a particular bovine.

> *Oh give me a home where the buffalo*
> *roam,*
> *Where the deer and the antelope play,*
> *Where seldom is heard a discouraging*
> *word,*
> *And the skies are not cloudy all day.*

> Refrain:
> *Home, home on the range,*
> *where the deer and the antelope play,*
> *Where seldom is heard a discouraging*
> *word,*
> *And the skies are not cloudy all day.*

> *Where the air is so pure, and the zephyrs*
> *so free,*
> *The breezes so balmy and light,*
> *That I would not exchange my home on*
> *the range,*
> *For all of the cities so bright.*

> Refrain

> *Oh, give me a land where the bright*
> *diamond sand*
> *Flows leisurely down the stream;*
> *Where the graceful white swan goes*
> *gliding along*
> *Like a maid in a heavenly dream.*

> Refrain

> *The red man was pressed from this part*
> *of the West,*
> *He's likely no more to return*
> *To the banks of Red River where seldom if*
> *ever*
> *Their flickering campfires burn.*

Hole in the Bucket

This is ideal for the drama queens in the group. Break your singing circle into two parts—Henrys and Lizas. If it can be males and females, all the better. This song is sung in alternating parts with escalating frustration.

The "Henrys" sing:
There's a hole in my bucket,
dear Liza, dear Liza.
There's a hole in my bucket,
dear Liza, a hole.

The "Lizas" sing:
Well fix it, dear Henry,
dear Henry, dear Henry.
Well fix it, dear Henry.
Dear Henry, fix it.

Henrys:
With what shall I fix it,
dear Liza, dear Liza?
With what shall I fix it,
dear Liza, with what?

Lizas:
With a straw-aw, dear Henry,
dear Henry, dear Henry.
With a straw-aw, dear Henry,
dear Henry, a straw.

H: The straw is too long. . .
L: Well cut it. . .
H: With what shall I cut it. . .
L: With an ax. . .
H: The ax is too dull. . .
L: Then sharpen it. . .
H: With what shall I sharpen it. . .
L: With a stone. . .
H: The stone is too dry. . .
L: Then wet it. . .
H: With what shall I wet it. . .
L: With water. . .
H: In what shall I fetch it. . .
L: With a bucket. . .

H: THERE'S A HOLE IN THE BUCKET!

Swing Low, Sweet Chariot

Spirituals are a soulful way to class up the repertoire. What beats "When the Saints Go Marching In," "Go, Tell It on the Mountain," "Rock My Soul (in the Bosom of Abraham)," and "He's Got the Whole World in His Hands"? My favorite is "Swing Low, Sweet Chariot" because it digs down deep but doesn't require the gravitas of "Amazing Grace."

Refrain:
Swing low, sweet chariot,
Coming for to carry me home,
Swing low, sweet chariot,
Coming for to carry me home.

I looked over Jordan, and what did I see?
Coming for to carry me home,
A band of angels coming after me,
Coming for to carry me home.

Refrain

If you get there before I do,
Coming for to carry me home,
Tell all my friends I'm coming, too.
Coming for to carry me home.

Refrain

I'm sometimes up and sometimes down,
Coming for to carry me home,
But still my soul feels heavenly bound,
Coming for to carry me home.

Refrain

Call for Backup

All these old, campy tunes aside, you can sing pretty much anything around the fire. The main prerequisite is that the majority of people know at least some of the songs or are game enough to fake it. When you range into more ambitious territory—spirituals, country songs, folk music, punk—it can be helpful to have accompaniment. A guitar or harmonica carrying the tune makes singers a bit more confident. Dobro, washboard, and Jew's harp have a Coen-brothers' cachet that goes over big at urban-hipster sing-alongs. Win friends among world music fans with a didgeridoo and Incan panpipes.

Percussion is also an excellent assistant. Clapping, stomping, thigh slapping, or banging a stick on your chair to keep the beat does wonders in herding all the singers toward the corral.

There are some instruments that really are no good around the campfire, however. An authentic Stradivarius, while an excellent fiddle, probably shouldn't spend time in the cold, dank night or near ember-spitting logs. Tubas are also not ideal. They just don't add a lot to the Baez-Dylan canon, and when tuba players suck in a big lungful of carbon monoxide, they tend to keel over, which is a party killer.

CHAPTER 6

Hot Vittles

*Don't worry about biting off more than you can chew; your
mouth is probably a whole lot bigger than you think.*

—cowboy wisdom

Fire Grub Fundamentals

Cowboys digging into tin plates piled high with fried steak and beans and biscuits and swigging mugs of black coffee spiked with hooch looked about as pleased as a human has a right to be. Who wouldn't? They didn't make the meal and they wouldn't clean up after. That job fell to Cookie, the chuck wagon chef. His day was longer and probably tougher than a cowpoke's. Up hours before anyone else, Cookie stirred the fire to life, set the sourdough biscuits to rise in the Dutch oven, and roasted and ground the coffee beans by hand. Then, after a day of choking on smoke and burning his fingers while preparing three squares, Cookie stayed up late, scraping the plates

and putting the chuck wagon to rights for the next day. There's a reason biscuit shooters and bean wranglers, as they were sometimes called behind their backs, were imperious drunks.

So before we launch into a conversation about chow, it's essential to recognize cooking over an outdoor fire for what it is—tedious, backbreaking, dirty, dangerous work. And yet, there's no better eating. When you introduce cooking into the patio fire mix, you need to have this reality in mind: We're out to channel the dreamy satisfaction of the cowboy, not the inebriated vexation of Cookie. We're out to relive evenings at Camp Wampum Stomp'em that ended with sticky, greasy fingers, not backaches, burn ointment, and piles of dishes.

Done right, roasting simple foods over fire enhances the sense of release from a complicated world. Done wrong, oh my.

If you want fire-brazed grub—and who doesn't?—without destroying your outdoor haven, keep these basic principles in mind.

1. Don't be afraid to mix high and low: Serving ash-infused edibles on fine china and providing linen napkins for finger food make for thrilling contrasts. (Just promise that you'll leave the clean-up 'til morning.)

2. Resist the urge to cook entire meals.
Think self-expression, not nourishment.

3. Revive simple techniques and nosh
recipes geared to five-year-olds.

4. Avoid foodie fads. An outdoor fire is not
the place for truffle oil and cilantro. It is the
place for Marshmallow Fluff and Cheez Whiz.

5. Forget the Joneses. Leave the gas
wok, the Sub-Zero fridge, and the six-burner
grill with Flavorizer bars to overachievers.

6. Think simple. Your fireplace should
accommodate a small pot or grill, but that's all.

The Dynamic Duo: Sticks and Foil

There's plenty of tempting paraphernalia for
outdoor cooks to sink their paychecks into—
rotisseries, Dutch ovens, tripods, spider skillets, racks, grills, baskets, chestnut roasters,
popcorn poppers, hot dog spears, long-handled
roasting forks of every possible configuration,
ergonomic pot clamps, and triangle dinner

bells. But ours is a stripped-down approach
that requires no more than sticks and aluminum foil: Whatever you can't skewer and
roast, you can wrap and bake. OK, this isn't
entirely true. It's impossible to skewer chili,
and wrapping it in foil is messy, but we're
reaching for a philosophy here, an ideal of fireside food that's equal parts Quaker and rebel.

A distinct advantage to these humble instruments is that they're cheap and they can
be used with any kind of fire setup. You don't
need a grill, a tripod, or a dingle stick from
which to hang pots. Most important, sticks
and foil encourage a do-it-yourself ethic, like
the open range itself.

The outside fireplace at its best is a chef-
free zone. No single person determines how
many raspberries go in your hobo pie or how
brown your biscuit will be, which doesn't mean
they can't mock you for your choices. (More on
that in a second.) The take-away here is that
in a stick-and-foil universe, everyone shoul-
ders the effort and shares the glory.

One final warning: Cooking in public
kindles the competitive spirit. If your weenie
burns or your marshmallow slides to a fiery
death, you'll hear about it. Fireside trash
talk—*Did your mother teach you to toast a
bun that way? What sort of hick heats the pickles?*—turns nosh fixing into a pro sport.

One Man, One Stick

The art of cooking with a stick over fire begins long before a match is lit, with the act of foraging for your tool. Depending on your slice of heaven, this can be as simple as looking under the trees in your yard or as complicated as looting a local park. I don't advocate harvesting boughs from trees, but pruning is a key time to plan ahead. Avoid branches of cherry, elderberry, and black locust trees, which have toxins in the foliage, twigs, or bark.

Ideally, the best all-around stick should be about two feet long, fairly straight, and about the width of your pinky finger, free from moss or loose bark. Gather several sticks on your rounds, with guests in mind or just to satisfy different moods and menus. I keep one with a blunt tip (that can be covered in foil) for biscuits. Another has a clean, whittled tip for spearing marshmallows, fruit, and hot dogs.

The longer your stick is separated from the mother tree, the more it dries out and is likely to catch fire along with your provisions. Consider soaking the cooking end in a pitcher of water overnight before a cookout as extra insurance.

When you've found a stick you love, make your claim on it. Wrap the handle in ribbon or plushy handlebar tape. It's nice for your cooking hand and keeps interlopers from trying to claim your prize twig. Eventually, you'll have to retire your magic wand. The only proper burial is to cast it into the flames—sans any inorganic adornments.

There are recipes that require store-bought backup in the form of manufactured roasting forks or bamboo or metal skewers for shish kebab. This is a great excuse to visit auction Web sites where lovely and strange vintage toasting forks in forged steel, iron, and copper are sometimes for sale. But that's outside our low-effort focus.

The challenge of stick cooking is location and patience. Novice stick cooks are eager, thrusting their booty into the flame, burning the outside while the inside remains positively cool. Take a page from barbecue experts who cook slowly over low heat. Also, a brush coating of vegetable oil helps keep meat, veggies, and fruit from drying out.

Below are three stick recipes from the old-timer's file: franks, biscuits, and s'mores.

COZY FRANKS

8 precooked hot dogs (or bratwurst, knockwurst, andouille, kielbasa, etc.)
4 ounces cheese, your favorite type, shredded or cut in strips (optional)
1 package refrigerated crescent rolls

MAKES 8 FRANKS

Wrap your hot dog with a triangle of dough as directed on the crescent roll package. You'll have the lovely croissant shape with a frankfurter sticking out on either end. If you like cheesy franks, begin by cutting a slit along the length of the hot dog and filling it with cheese before creating the bun. Then spear your hot dog and roast it over the fire.

The individual with the most discipline ends up with the best dog. Constantly rotating it over coals is the only way to bake the roll all the way through without burning it. This can take as long as 15 minutes. Avoid direct flame, which will char the outside.

If patience is not your virtue, roast the wiener on one stick and warm a regular, packaged bun with another. This only takes about 5 minutes, tops. It's best to spear your hot dog at an end, so you can expose the greatest surface area to direct heat. There are metal spears with wooden handles made for this purpose (see Resources, page 130).

Dress with squeeze ketchup and mustard. A flame-broiled dog doesn't need anything else. Serve with no-frills potato chips on flimsy paper plates that can go straight into the fire when you're finished. Wash down with grape soda or cans of beer.

STICKY BISCUITS

2 ¼ cups biscuit mix (such as Bisquick)
⅔ cup milk
½ cup cheddar cheese (optional)
Butter, jam, cinnamon, etc., for toppings

MAKES 8 BISCUITS

Find a stick, one per cook, about 2 feet long and ½ inch thick. Slightly fatter or skinnier is no problem—we're not doing heart surgery. Rinse off the end and wrap it in foil.

In a medium-sized bowl, stir mix and milk together until you have a soft dough. Turn onto a surface sprinkled with Bisquick. Knead about 10 times. Flatten the dough, and, with a sharp knife, cut it in half. Cut the halves in half, and cut each quarter in half. You'll have eight fairly uniform clumps of dough.

Make a ball of dough, about the size of a plum. Push the foil end of the stick into the dough far enough so it is secure, but not all the way through doughnut-style. It should be shaped like the tall bearskin hats of British guardsmen. (Burn it, and the resemblance is complete.)

Toast over the coals until golden brown, about 10 minutes. If, when you begin to slide the biscuit off the stick, it feels gooey inside, let it spend more time in the heat of the fire, but not too near the coals. Once it's cooked, pull off the biscuit and fill the cavity with butter and jam, or butter and cinnamon sugar, or peanut butter and honey—whatever floats your biscuit.

For a savory option, add ½ cup shredded cheddar cheese to the dough, and cut the mix back to 2 cups. When they're cooked, try dripping melted garlic butter in the hole.

Stick biscuits require practice and can be a source of minor humiliation. Your fellow firesiders aren't going to go easy when your big glob of dough loses its purchase. Continually rotating your stick helps in the battle with gravity.

Tramping with Mr. Stay Puft

The marshmallow sits at the pinnacle of the campfire food pyramid, above whiskey, wieners, and baked beans. Thousands of years ago in Egypt and Rome, marsh mallow was a flowering plant hauled from salty marshes and used in health remedies. But them days is long gone. Today, the marshmallow is a marvel of engineering: corn syrup and starch, sugar, water, gelatin, tetrasodium pyrophosphate, artificial flavor, and Blue #1—jet-puffed and extruded in a snow-white tubelet. Fresh from the bag, marshmallows feel like powdered rubber and smell like tooth decay. But toast them over a flame, and smoky-sweet miracle goo is born.

In many ways, there's no improving on the fire-browned marshmallow, and yet there is a constant effort to do so. (I'm no exception.) One of the great mysteries of the twentieth century is exactly who decided to add even more sugar to the mix in the form of graham crackers and chocolate. But the creators of s'mores foresaw the rightness of the combination—and their audacity is honored around campfires year-round.

The first published recipe for s'mores probably appeared in *Tramping and Trailing with the Girl Scouts,* a Girl Scout handbook, in 1927.

While the sandwich approach is the model technique, the makers of the Rolla Roaster, a telescoping toasting fork (see Resources, page 130), offer a s'mores variation that shows the sugar puff off to tasty advantage.

In this version, you toast the marshmallow until it's golden brown and then roll it in mini-chocolate chips. (No flamers with this recipe. Chips don't stick well to the hard, charred shell.) Then delicately rotate the chipped-up marshy back over the fire for a second or two. Once the chocolate begins to melt, take it from the fire and roll it in crushed graham crackers. To my mind, the ratio of chocolate and cookie pieces to marshmallow in this version is superb.

There are so many innovations on the original s'mores recipe that Girl Scouts founder Juliette Gordon Low has probably rolled clear free of her grave. But all that delectable trial and error has yielded some worthy amendments, including caramel (try caramel syrup rather than caramel squares, which don't soften up enough), crunchy peanut butter, Nutella (hazelnut and cocoa spread), and ground cashews.

While we're tipping a sacred cow, don't feel locked into the graham cracker thing. Gingersnaps, for example, are delicious with chocolate and marshmallows. Of all the s'mores variations, in my opinion, none entirely dusts the original, except perhaps this roasted peach with white chocolate version.

PEACH S'MORES

4 luscious ripe peaches, pitted and halved
1 white chocolate candy bar, about
  1 square per peach
8 large marshmallows
4 graham crackers, $\frac{1}{2}$ cracker per
  open-faced s'more

MAKES 8 S'MORES

On a stick, roast a peach half. As it warms, peel the skin away (it will slide right off). Toss the skin into the flames. The skinless peach should be golden brown in about 7 minutes.

Place the cooked peach on a plate, flat side up. Top with white chocolate. While the chocolate melts over the hot peach, roast your marshmallow to a light brown. Then place it on the chocolate. Top with half a graham cracker, pressing down so the marshmallow goes gooey. Flip the whole thing over and devour.

Some friends top their peach s'mores with another graham cracker, so it's like a sandwich, but I think that makes it harder to eat. Plus, the balance of tangy peach, smooth chocolate, and sweet marshmallow is best with half a cracker.

BLOW, DON'T THROW:

From the It's All Fun and Games Until Someone Loses an Eye Department: Don't wave your flaming marshmallow around to make it go out. Blow on it. Otherwise you could launch a flying projectile of red-hot trouble.

Full Metal Packet

Foil cookery has the advantage of thriving in the face of neglect, at least when compared to the stick. Throw everything in your pouch, seal it up, toss it on the coals, flip it, or forget about it. The most common foil food is probably potatoes, baked or chopped with onions, garlic, butter, and seasoning. But an entire culinary canon can be wrapped in foil and cooked over fire.

Ideally, use heavy-duty aluminum foil (or double sheets), since regular foil is more easily punctured by sharp points in the fire. Also, wide sheets—eighteen inches—allow for more freedom in creating packages, like the spacious pouch you'll need for Gypsy Popcorn.

Generally, use a piece of foil at least twice as long as you want the completed food package to be. Lay it flat, shiny side in. If you're worried the food may stick, spray the foil with nonstick oil spray. Place your edibles in the center. Fold the long edges of the foil over, so they overlap and cover the food. Press the top sheets together and fold to create a seam of about a half inch. Fold over two more times to seal the seam. Repeat on the sides.

When cooking meat and fish, seal packages so there's almost no space between foil and food. Close contact between food, foil, and fire aids browning. To keep from burning meat or fish, layer the bottom of the pouch with lemon slices and don't flip the package.

In cooking vegetables, it's better to leave air space like a tent. In this way, the pouch works like a pressure cooker, steaming the foods. If you double your foil, the inside sheet remains ash-free and can be used as a serving dish. For control and accident prevention, it's best to keep serving sizes small in foil cookery, but the recipes that follow provide foil-cooked party nosh for small groups.

COWBOY NACHOS

3 big handfuls of scoop-size Fritos
  corn chips
1 cup shredded cheddar and Monterey
  Jack cheese
1 small can baked beans
Chopped jalapeños, onion, peppers,
  or tomatoes (optional), for garnish

MAKES APPETIZER-SIZE SERVINGS FOR 4

Coat a wide piece of foil that is twice as long as
it is wide with vegetable oil cooking spray. Put
a few handfuls of chips in the center, top with
half the cheese, and scoop beans with a slotted
spoon (so that much of the juice drains away)
onto the cheese. Top beans with the rest of
the cheese and any additional garnish. I like to
top mine with jalapeños or salsa verde, which
provides a spicy counterpoint to the sweet
beans and salty chips. Raw, chopped onions
work well, too.

TEMPERATURE TANTRUMS:
Unlike charcoal, which offers predict-
able heat, wood is more of a crap-
shoot. That's why restaurant kitchens
use charcoal with wood-chip accents
in many "wood-fired" stoves.

GYPSY POPCORN

1 teaspoon oil
2 tablespoons popcorn
1 tablespoon butter, plus extra melted
  butter to drizzle over the popped corn
Salt and paprika

MAKES APPETIZER-SIZE SERVINGS FOR 2

In the middle of an 18- by 30-inch piece of aluminum foil, add the oil and popcorn. Top with butter. Bring foil corners together to make a pouch. Secure the edges of the foil but leave plenty of room for the popcorn to expand. Attach the pouch at the end of a stick, like hobo luggage, and hold the pouch over the hot coals. Shake constantly until all the popcorn has popped. Add butter, salt, and paprika to taste.

NO-CRUST APPLE PIE

4 tablespoons butter, 1 for each apple
4 teaspoons brown sugar
1 teaspoon cinnamon
1 teaspoon nutmeg
Dash of ginger (optional)
4 apples (tart fruit works best)

MAKES 4 "APPLE PIES"

Create a paste of soft butter, brown sugar, cinnamon, and nutmeg. A dash of powdered ginger is also a nice addition.

Core the apples. Fill each hole with one-quarter of the butter paste. Wrap each apple in foil tightly. Warm over coals. After 10 minutes, you'll have warm, crispy apples; wait 15 minutes for hot, soft apples.

Irons in the Fire

Only one tool combines the flexibility and individuality of the stick with the ease and versatility of foil: the pie iron. So simple and yet so inspired, it ranks up there with the wheel and the back-scratcher. Also known as pie shams, sandwich cookers, and toasty-ties, a pie iron is a hinged cast-iron or aluminum press, about the size of a sandwich, that looks like a waffle iron with long handles.

The pie iron is by no means an exclusively American device. There are equivalents around the world. In street stalls in Australia, South Africa, and Indonesia, pressed and grilled sandwiches are made in similar irons called jaffle irons or, simply, "jaffles." Panini grills operate in the same way in Italy and around Europe, but usually aren't as portable. In the United States, pie irons have been around in their present incarnation since the sixties, but early predecessors dating back to the forties are still kicking around.

Depending on where you grew up and your family's idea of a good time in the outdoors, you may or may not be a member of the pie iron tribe. But make no mistake, this unassuming instrument has a cultlike following. True fans exchange recipes in campgrounds, at fairs, and over the Internet. They debate the merits of aluminum versus cast iron as if their lives, not a sandwich, depended on it. They establish strict (if tongue-in-cheek) codes of conduct, including in at least one case a toasty-tie oath that bars cooks from overstuffing the pie, neglecting "the baby," or shouting "iron-free!" instead of "iron clear!" Get the picture?

I lived in Colorado for my first eighteen years, which included a lot of camping, and never ran into one of these marvels. Across the country, Ray Frick, a banjo player out of Philadelphia, grew up on camping and pie irons. For several years, he was part of an ambitious pie-making duo that churned out thousands of hobo pies during the weeklong Appalachian String Band Festival in West Virginia. So complete is his dedication to the art, he named his old-time music quartet the Hobo Pie Band. Since I'll remain a novice well into my first decade of pie iron cooking, Frick supplied much of our expert perspective.

The Five Steps of Pie Iron Cooking

The heart of pie iron cuisine is a five-step sandwich-making process.

1. Begin with a foundation, usually a slice of buttered bread, butter side down in the pie iron. Brushing bread with olive oil works as well, depending on the recipe.

2. Spoon your filling onto the center of the bread—cooked meat, cheese, vegetables, peanut butter, jelly, canned pie fruit, whatever. Frick's approach is to pile the filling high in the center of the bread to avoid seep around the edges. Avoid overstuffing the iron, since as food heats, it expands and can lead to a blowout.

3. Place a second slice of bread on top, butter side up.

4. Close the pie iron and latch the handles. Trim off any bread hanging outside the iron. This is a good way to get rid of bread crusts, which many pie aficionados don't like. The goal is to create a good seal.

5. Hold the iron over the fire, turning it until the pie is golden brown. Coals or flame, it doesn't really matter to your pie iron, which makes things easy. It's OK to open your pie iron to check if your pie is cooked. Tap the outside of the iron to avoid "stickage."

These five steps are the foundation of an entire food culture, the means to a daunting array of cuisines from goat cheese turnovers, fruit pies, and empanadas to calzones, chocolate croissants, and Northwoods pasties. Who needs a Weber?

While bread is the preferred foundation, you can create pudgie pies and mountain pies (as they are also known) using egg roll wrappers, puff pastry, piecrusts, and soft tortillas—anything that will cook up and form a seal on the outside edge. Pie irons can also be used as skillets to fry eggs, potatoes, and the like.

Frick sprays Pam on his irons. He only cooks with cast-iron versions (no aluminum). He prefers round pie irons, which, after more than 12,000 hobo pies, he says maintain the best seal. Finally, he claims the Cadillac of pie irons is made by Rome Industries, a family-run shop in Peoria, Illinois (see Resources, page 130).

The sky's the limit with the pie iron. Next I've included a few standout hobo recipes, but only as a way to sharpen your appetite and inspire your own culinary inventions.

P.B.M.B.

A peanut butter and jelly sandwich grilled in a pie iron is sublime in its simplicity and tough to improve on. But the P.B.M.B. (peanut butter, marshmallow, and banana) is a worthy challenger.

Spread plenty of butter on the cooking sides of white bread. Elvis would want it that way. Then on the inside, spread peanut butter and Marshmallow Fluff, almost to the edges. Add a layer of sliced bananas, seal, and grill. A dash of cinnamon is to die for.

SPAMMY

Well before spam was a dirty word for junk e-mail, it was a luncheon meat; Hormel spiced ham in a can was born in 1937 (with the *sp* from *spiced* and the *am* from *ham*). Frick remembers Spam hobo pies from family camping trips in the sixties. For these, he combines Spam with Cabot aged Vermont cheddar cheese, chopped tomatoes, and onions on white or wheat bread. This sandwich is named for Spammy, the Spam spokes-pig on George Burns and Gracie Allen's forties radio show.

PHILLY CHEESE STEAK PIE

In advance, sauté chopped onions, peppers, and mushrooms until soft. Then fry up some thinly sliced, tender beef until brown but not crispy or burned. (Conceivably, you could do all this sautéing in an open-faced pie iron, but that's close quarters.) Combine steak, vegetables, and cheese on the bread of your choice. I prefer provolone, but Cheez Whiz is another authentic choice. Also, Frick adds a "gentle squeeze" of pizza sauce from a squeeze bottle. Remember to resist the urge to overstuff your pie. You can always make a second and a third.

LITTLE ITALY

Brush olive oil on the outside of the bread. (Garlic-infused olive oil is really nice here but dangerously foodie.) Spread your favorite pizza sauce or marinara on one slice, and top it with shredded mozzarella cheese, pepperoni slices, crumbled sausage, or anything you like on your pizza.

Inspired by panini, Frick makes his hobo pies with Italian ciabatta bread brushed with olive oil, topped with sun-dried tomatoes, fresh mozzarella, and prosciutto. A far cry from his early Spam days.

Pie Iron Care

When you're finished, wipe out the inside of your pie iron. Never use soapy water with cast iron; just allow the surface to season over time.

Pie irons are also available in cast aluminum versions. These are lighter, easier to maneuver, and easier to clean, but not the choice of serious pie people. Either way, never wash the outside of the irons. Just pop them in a plastic shopping bag after they have cooled to keep the char from getting all over the place. A clean pie iron is an unhappy pie iron.

Pie Iron Entertaining

If you plan a group pie iron cookout, chop up lots of condiments in advance to inspire the proceedings. You'll want the usual suspects such as shredded cheese, chopped onions, garlic, scallions, parsley, green peppers, and tomatoes, but sprinkle in a few surprises, such as jalapenos, pepperoncini, and sweet pickles.

Whistle Wetters

Whiskey is the true firewater, the choice of those seeking an unalloyed fire night. But not everybody wants hair on their chest. Bottles of beer are a softer touch and play well with sodas in a tub of ice. If you must drink wine, serve up saucy cabernet in jam jars to maintain the low-culture pretense. While a bartender is completely out of the question, a do-it-yourself cocktail is another matter, especially one that tastes like it's good for you, such as Lemon Aid.

BOOZE SLANG:

The word *firewater* probably comes from when traders selling whiskey to Native Americans poured it onto the fire to demonstrate its flammability, as in "So strong you can start your barbecue with it!"

LEMON AID

Ice (about 2 ice trays)
2 tablespoons sugar
2 large lemons
3 ounces ice-cold vodka

MAKES ABOUT 4 SHORT COCKTAILS

Add ice to a 32-ounce, wide-mouth water bottle until it's about half full. Add sugar. Slice lemons into eighths, squeezing the juice into the bottle, and then add the slices until packed tightly. (With smaller lemons, halve or quarter and use more. Lemons should fill the water bottle to the top.) Pour in the vodka. Seal and start shaking.

When your arms are tired, hand off the container to a friend. He or she shakes, passes it on, and so on. By the fourth shaker, it's probably ready to taste. Add more sugar or vodka to taste, and shake until ambrosia. Share the bottle or serve in old-time stainless steel coffee mugs that have a great Adirondack feel (but don't keep coffee or tea warm). Another serving option is to have guests bring their own water bottles and make their own Lemon Aid.

This recipe works with muddled mint, ice, sugar, limes, and rum as well (aka a mojito).

COWBOY COFFEE

Cowboy coffee is one of those beverages that may be more fun to talk about than to sip, but there's something to be said for bucking the whole Frappuccino scene with such an authentic and gritty option, especially around an outdoor fire.

The phrase *cowboy coffee* refers to a brewing technique—adding grinds directly to a pot of boiling water—birthed of necessity on the range. There appears to be no definitive approach, but in each variation, brewers are trying to tackle two challenges: loose grinds and bitterness.

Before anyone goes all snobby and cranks the Gaggia, keep in mind that in the days before the Civil War, nearly all chuck wagon cooks carried green coffee beans and roasted them in frying pans over the fire immediately before grinding and brewing. That rivals most high-end coffee joints for freshness.

GAUCHO ETIQUETTE:
Whenever a cowboy went to fill his coffee cup and heard the words "Man at the pot!" he was obligated to serve refills to all who requested them.

1 quart boiling water
³/₄ cup coarsely ground coffee
1 eggshell, broken up
¹/₄ cup cold water

MAKES 4 CUPS

Bring a quart of water to a boil in a Dutch oven or an aluminum coffeepot nestled in hot coals. Add the coffee and eggshell. Once it boils again, immediately remove the pot from the fire. Let the coffee stand covered for 2 minutes. Slowly add the cold water to settle the grounds at the bottom. Serve right away. The longer this coffee sits around, the stronger and more bitter it gets. Cowboy coffee is not good to the last sip. Be prepared to pour the last cup onto the mulch pile.

Some cooks strain out the coffee grounds, which is strictly tenderfoot. Others don't add cold water or eggshell, but are content to let the grounds settle for a few minutes. Sugar, milk, and a shot of hard spirits help take some of the sting out of this brew.

Resources

Nearly everything described in this book can easily be found in home and garden stores, fire supply shops, or other specialty stores in most cities. But there are a few special cases for which you need to go directly to the source, by phone or online.

Fire Starting

Magnifying glass, bow-drill, hand drill, and flint and steel fire-starter kits and instructional videos
Midwest Native Skills Institute
Cleveland, Ohio
(888) 886-5592; survivalschool.com

Boutique Wood

Juniper and piñon firewood
New Mexico Piñon Company, Inc.
Alto, New Mexico
(888) 297-4067; chimenea-wood.com

Piñon Pine "Bug Off" Firewood
Beaver Creek Outfitters, LLC
Beaver, Wisconsin
(920) 680-9663; beavercreekoutfitter.com

Hotsticks
Gish Logging, Inc.
Fort Loudon, Pennsylvania
(717) 369-2151; hotsticks.net

Pitchwood starters
Lightning Nuggets, Inc.
Davenport, Washington
(800) 468-4487; lightningnuggets.com

Moon Gazing

See free images of the moon taken by the *Galileo* spacecraft en route to Jupiter:
astrogeology.usgs.gov/projects/
browsethesolarsystem/moon.html

Ghost Stories

The Bookcase Ghost: A Storyteller's Collection of Wisconsin Ghost Stories by Elizabeth Matson and Stuart Stotts (Midwest Traditions).

I'm Not Scared: Scary Songs and Stories, Ages 8 and Up, recording of stories and songs performed by Stuart Stotts.

Book and tape/CD available from Stuart Stotts at stuart.stotts.com; (608) 241-9143.

Toasting Tools

Rolla Roaster
Working in a lean-to shop attached to his single-wide trailer, Bob Holzer invented this rotating, telescoping fork with wooden handles in 1980. It's an inexpensive and no-frills tool that feels like something you'd be thrilled to discover in your parent's basement.

Orofino, Idaho
(800) 480-4308; rollaroaster.com

Hot dog roasting sticks
These are perfect for franks, because they allow you to roast the entire hot dog surface on one long tine. Like the Rolla Roaster, these 48-inch metal hot dog roasting sticks with wood handles are handmade in small batches, in this case by self-described survivors of corporate downsizing.

(937) 806-1518; hotdogsticks.com

Cowboy Coffee

Although cowboy coffee refers to a brewing method, there is a brand of coffee associated with nineteenth-century cattle drives: Arbuckles'. In 1865, a pair of Pittsburgh grocer-brothers, John and Charles Arbuckle, patented a process for roasting and then coating coffee beans with an egg-and-sugar glaze. The glaze helped seal in the flavor and aroma, and made roasting on the range unnecessary. Chuck wagons were soon fully loaded with pound bags of Arbuckles' coffee, which came (and still do) with a free peppermint inside.

Arbuckle Coffee Roasters
Tuscon, Arizona
(800) 533-8278; arbucklecoffee.com

Acknowledgments

This book is the result of countless nights around an open fire—my own and those of the people who generously shared their experiences and smarts with me. I am indebted to every person who eventually succumbed to my pestering—in particular, survival educator and fire master Aaron Huey, food writer Sara Dickerman, culinary sage Christie Withers, storyteller Stuart Stotts, banjo-playing pie iron master Ray Frick, and my dad, whose beautiful story about hunting duck and then cooking it over a hibachi one misty morning during the Korean War never made it in the manuscript—until now. Also, special thanks are due to those people with backyard fireplaces who opened their homes to me, especially Dan and Anne McGowan, Charlotte Behnke, and Jonna Bracken and Jamie Corn, who graciously permitted us to take photos. Thanks also to my editors at Sasquatch Books: Gary Luke, who signed me up for the entirely pleasant experience of playing with fire and getting paid for it, and Heidi Schuessler and Terry Stella, who minded the details.

—L.W.